ENTER, WITH TORCHES

Recollections of a Grumpy Old Editor

PARK BURROUGHS

CONTENTS

Foreword

In December 1970, I signed on as a copy boy at the Sun-Sentinel in Fort Lauderdale, Fla., at $2 an hour. Teaching jobs were hard to find, and I needed to pay rent and buy groceries.

The news business was new to me, not that I had much to do with the news. Mainly, I ran copy from the editors up to the composing room, and proofs from there back to the editors, and took orders from the reporters and fetched their dinners at White Castle. But just being around the commotion of a newsroom, where journalists were frantically scrounging information about plane crashes and murders and bank robberies was romantic. Soon, I was infected with the news virus.

I ended up a year later as a sports writer at the Observer-Reporter in Washington, Pa., and never left. Eventually, I was in charge, and have been so now for more than 20 years. Along the way, I did a lot of writing. But it didn't become regular until something came along to change newspapers forever and threaten their very existence: the Internet.

In 2005, I began writing a Web log, or blog, a daily Web posting designed to keep me in touch with our readers – not just the traditional newspaper readers but the new ones, the ones who don't even buy the newspaper but read it online. Called "Grumpy Old Editor," I answered reader complaints in a smarmy, cantankerous way that I wouldn't dare try over the phone or face to face. And I offered my own gripes, on a daily basis. I thought that I would never run out of things to complain about, but I did.

The blog was successful. I had started a conversation with readers that is not possible in a printed newspaper. Sure, people can write letters to the editor complaining about what we write, but on paper, that is the end of the conversation. On the Web, we could chat ad nauseam.

The online audience was different than our traditional newspaper readership. Younger and more in tune with social trends, online readers were unlikely to complain about edgy topics, vulgar language and satire they did not understand. The blog was an ideal place to experiment with new types of newspaper writing.

A part of my blog was called the "Catfish Creek of Consciousness." Catfish Creek is a dirty little stream that courses unnoticed through my adopted hometown, which was called Catfish Camp in the 18th century. My idea was to provide online readers with four or five paragraphs on some thought that would lead to another thought the next day. Online comments from readers would change the course of the narrative, which might go on for weeks. But the Catfish Creek of Consciousness suffered from a drought of participation and was reduced to a trickle. Then I decided to resurrect a type of writing common in newspapers of a century ago: the serialized story.

Sitting at my desk in the newsroom early on a Monday morning, I would dredge my brain for a memory and start typing a story, not knowing how it would end or how many days it would take to get there. When I finished that story, I started another. The reaction to these experiments – fiction, or strings of anecdotes – was dismal. Defeated, I considered abandoning the blog, but decided to write one last story: a story about failure and how it makes one a stronger person. I called it "Watertown," in which I described how I flunked out of prep school and broke my father's heart.

Suddenly, I had the attention of my Internet readers. The stories kept coming, and still do. Some of the tales have been not about my life but about local characters, now dead and long forgotten, who had changed the course of our lives. The tales in this volume are those that received the most comments by this new audience, the many who browse this newspaper not the old-fashion way, but on their computers, all around this nation and the world, far away from Catfish Creek.

All the stories in this book were first introduced with a warning to readers that what they were about to read was true, as much as my faulty memory could recall; and that some of the names have been changed to avoid embarrassment; and that although I knew how the story would begin, I did not know how long it would go on or how it would end.

Just like life.

Park Burroughs

AUTHOR PARK BURROUGHS IS SEATED AT
RIGHT IN THIS 1962 PHOTO OF HIS SEVENTH-
GRADE HOMEROOM.

CHAPTER ONE

Bronxville Days

We didn't actually live in Bronxville, N.Y. We had a Bronxville mailing address, but the town itself was just one square mile – "Bronxville Proper," they called it – and the people who lived in that square were either rich or old, or both. Bronxville was where our fathers got on the train to go to work in New York City. It was where we went to church: Episcopal, Congregational, Catholic or Dutch Reformed, your choice. It was where we went to the movies, and to buy model cars, and to eat banana splits and to ride our decorated bikes in the Memorial Day parade.

There was a tall building in the center of town – the Hotel Gramatan. It was where all the rich widows lived. It was a great place to go trick-or-treating. You could see the sign atop the hotel – made from red light bulbs – for miles. One night some teenagers got up on the roof and knocked out some of the lights so that the sign read, "HOT GRAMA." I remember my mother telling a friend how hilarious that was, and then catching me eavesdropping, changed her mind and called it disgraceful vandalism.

Before moving to Bronxville, we had been Catholics. Back in West Haven, Conn., I remember going to classes taught by terrifying nuns. I don't remember much about it, other than being told by them that someone named "Mary" was my real mother. I deduced from this that the woman at my house who raised me, "Irene" as she was called by others, was a fraud.

Anyway, for some reason when we moved to Bronxville, or near it, we didn't go to the Catholic church but rather the big, fancy Episcopal one. In my twisted 9-year-old brain, I figured that we had been promoted.

I'll never forget the humiliation my parents put me through in that church. I had worn my good shoes to school on Friday and changed into my gym shoes, then forgot to change back and left my good shoes in my locker.

"Get dressed for church, young man," I was told Sunday morning. "But I can't go to church today because I left my good shoes in my locker at school."

The parents were tired of this excuse. "Then you'll go in your sneakers," they said.

I was inordinately fashion conscious for a boy my age. The idea of dressing in a gray flannel suit and filthy high-top white Keds was repulsive.

They dragged me to church. I felt like a clown. I was mortified.

I never forgot my good shoes at school again.

Children do not invent bad behavior; they learn it from older kids. And we had our share of bad influences in the neighborhood.

Some of the tricks we learned were relatively harmless, like the Jar of Death. If you happened to have a really bad case of rotten-egg farts, we learned from Billy Higgins that you could capture and store one indefinitely in a tightly sealed peanut butter jar. The Jar of Death could then be taken to an appropriate event, such as a birthday party, where its effect could be best appreciated.

Other stunts were downright stupid and dangerous. I knew better than to imitate two older boys who liked to stalk each other around the neighborhood with bows and arrows. The arrows had target tips but were still capable of penetrating flesh, which they did on at least one occasion, the victim proudly displaying his wound to all who would look.

I foolishly learned and practiced another stunt, though. In winter, when the streets were covered in snow and oil delivery to homes frequent, we would sneak behind a fuel truck as it was leaving a driveway and grab hold of the back bumper and slide down the street of the soles of our boots.

Older kids would visit the city and buy firecrackers in Chinatown. They'd set off whole packs of these. One day Jimmy Paulus and I found several unexploded crackers and decided to put one into a hollowed-out tree stump with some toy soldiers and light it and see what happened. We did, and ran a few yards away and waited, and nothing happened. So Jimmy went back to the stump and looked in, and that's when it exploded.

Something flew into his eye. The next day, it was still red and his vision blurry, so he had to tell his Mom. His eye was permanently damaged. He had to get glasses.

We were just 9 years old. You could say that we didn't know any better. But we did, and I don't think I've ever gotten over the shame, the guilt and remorse of that incident. My parents didn't punish me. They knew it wasn't necessary. A lesson was learned, and for Jimmy, it was the hard way.

CHRISTMAS, 1957. WHEN WE MOVED TO THE
HOUSE IN BRONXVILLE, THERE WERE JUST FOUR
OF US: MY PARENTS AND MY SISTER PAT AND I.

Maybe you've experimented with Google Earth on your computer. You type in an address and you zoom in from space to the exact spot on the planet you've selected and see it – perhaps the neighborhood of your youth – as a bird would, or more accurately, as a satellite does.

And so I visit our old house, at the corner of Millard and Ellison. The house and the whole neighborhood look pretty much as they did 50 years ago, except for the giant highway that now slashes through what used to be our wilderness to the east. I trace the streets along which I used to pedal my bike, past Public School No. 8, past the stationery store where we used to spend our money on Three Musketeers bars and baseball cards and Mad Magazines, past Gristede's Grocery, where we bought the white beans for our pea shooters, down onto Palmer Avenue, across from Sarah Lawrence College, where all those barefoot beatnik girls studied, and on to the Bronx River.

Surely, my parents must have been aware of how far I went on my bicycle, and which roads and busy intersections I crossed – without a helmet, I might add, as there were no such things in those days – on my way to town some two miles distant.

The river – more of a creek, really – was damned a few hundred yards upstream, and the pond was where my friends and I with bamboo poles fished on lazy summer days for bluegills and catfish.

I can smell it now, that memory: pond water, fish slime and earthworms. I can almost feel the sun on my shoulders, picture my scabby knees, watch my child hands, black under the fingernails, baiting the hook. I hear the rush of water over the dam, the barking of dogs taken for walks, the whoosh of cars on the nearby parkway.

This was happiness defined, being 9 or 10 years old and to have all this place as a playground, and to be without worry and fear, and to be so far removed from the ugly realities of life.

My mother held a match to the wine cork, which blackened and released a thin stream of dark, aromatic smoke. She held the cork until the black area cooled, then gripped my chin firmly, drew a moustache across my lip, darkened my eyebrows and added long sideburns.

"There you go, my little Mexican man," she said.

Fixing a sombrero on my head and draping a serape around my shoulders, she said, "You keep bundled up tonight, it's cold out there."

She put her hands on my shoulders and held me still for a moment, contemplating her creation.

"You're getting to be such a big boy. This stuff wouldn't even fit you last year. And I guess this will be your last trick-or-treat. You'll be too old for this next year."

The doorbell rang and I bounded downstairs. "You wait for your sister!" she yelled after me. "Aw, Ma, she's 8 years old, she can go herself," I said, but I knew it was of no use.

Jimmy was at the door, dressed as a Texas Ranger. Behind him stood two smaller children, one in a white sheet with holes cut for eyes, the other in a box with a cardboard disk for a hat – Speedy Alka Seltzer. "Sorry," Jimmy said. "My mom made me take them along."

My mother handed us brown paper grocery bags, and, kissing my sister on the forehead said, "Don't take this scarf off and stick close to your brother, and don't eat all the candy before you get home."

It was just after 6 o'clock, Monday, Oct. 31, 1960. A sliver of golden moon hung in the black sky. We shuffled down the walk, marched under the streetlight at the corner of Millard and Ellison and passed into the darkness, stumbling on the sidewalk, the cracks and buckled concrete reaching up to catch the toes of our shoes. We bounced like moths from lighted porch to lighted porch, shivering in the consuming black of night between them. Gusts of wind sent dry maple leaves skittering across the street like frightened animals and fanned an eerie red glow in piles of leaf ash at the curb. The obscure shapes of other children, their voices wafting on the breeze, passed us on the opposite side of the street.

We clambered up steps and rang bells and waited in the flickering orange light of jack-o-lanterns. Muffled noises, homey sounds of television, creaking floors and barking dogs came through the doors, which swung open, emitting the different smells of people's suppers. A woman held a bowl of Baby Ruths before us. Wait, she said. Let me guess who you are. She knew us all except Tommy Gagan, who had caught up with us along the avenue, wrapped from head to toe in strips of sheets like a mummy.

At another house, on a lonely stretch of Birchbrook Road, an old man extended a basket of apples in one hand and a bowl of pennies in the other. "Take a big handful," he urged. "Go on, dig in." Copper rained in our paper bags. We sauntered down the middle of the road, munching the apples and tossing the cores into the woods.

Halloween would never be the same after that night. For me, the spooky magic would be gone, replaced by mischief and hoarding from the candy mine of the Hotel Gramatan. And it wasn't too many years later that Halloween was ruined, buy sick people putting needles in candy bars and razor blades in apples, and by municipalities that replaced trick-or-treat with parties held not on Oct. 31 but on whatever day seemed convenient to adults, and by the adults who hijacked the simple observance and made it an opportunity to party.

Building stuff. Sleeping out. These were our responses to boredom.
Sometimes we would even build stuff to sleep in. We'd find large
cardboard appliance boxes, tape them together, cut windows and doors
in them, attach old sheets as awnings, then drag our sleeping bags into
the makeshift mansion for the night.

Although the front yard with its rose and tulip beds was off-limits
to us kids, my parents allowed us to do as we pleased in our backyard,
which was not visible from the street. There we dug underground forts,
built huge, unfloatable rafts and assembled rockets from cardboard
storage barrels. I built a shack from old doors and sheets of plywood,
covered it in tarpaper to keep out the rain, and painted a skull and
crossbones above the entrance. An extension cord from the garage
provided electricity for a light and a radio. It was the perfect clubhouse
and a place to camp out at any time of year, but it didn't last long.

One night in early March, four of us were spending the night in
the shed. My father came out to say goodnight and told us to quiet
down and not to leave the shed. But we did anyway. It was a mild
night, but snow still covered the ground. We walked toward town, then
climbed a hill and started lobbing snowballs toward passing cars below.
The snowballs weren't having much effect, so we packed them hard
and added gravel. One of the missiles scored a direct hit on a driver's-
side door, and the car braked to a stop. We ran laughing back into the
woods for a few minutes, then emerged again and resumed our assault.

Suddenly, something grabbed the collar of my coat, and I was
yanked to my feet. The driver had stopped his car, then circled around
and crept up into the woods and caught Neil Heiner and I by the scruff
of our necks. The other two kids took off like startled fawns. The man
dragged us down the hill and put us into the backseat of his Rambler
station wagon, along with his own wide-eyed, terrified children. He
made us tell him where we lived, then drove us to our houses, called

WE BUILT STUFF, LIKE THIS GO-KART, USING A

LAWN-MOWER ENGINE, WAGON WHEELS

AND PLYWOOD.

our parents and told them what we'd done.

The punishment I received was severe and wide-ranging. I was forced to rat out my fleet-footed friends. I was deprived of allowance and television and sleeping out for months. Worst of all, I was ordered to tear down the shack.

You'd think that would have been enough to teach me never to deceive my parents or do something really stupid like that again, but I was, regrettably, a slow learner.

Student self-esteem must have been a concern to educators even back in the 1950s, because all of a sudden "F" disappeared as an option for teachers marking up report cards at Public School No. 8. A's, B's, C's and D's were left untouched, but F's, which stood for "Failure" (or maybe ("Flunky") had to go. F's were replaced with I's, which stood for "Improvement needed."

When our teacher, Miss Cynthia Heinitz, handed us our report cards on the last day of school, I was expecting my grades to be poor. But I never thought my report card would have more I's on it than "Mississippi." I couldn't get up the courage to give the report card to my mother, so I tossed it behind a pile of lumber in our garage.

That evening, when asked to produce it. I tried several approaches: "We didn't get report cards this year"; "Oh, yeah, we got them, but I must have dropped it on my way home from school"; "It might have fallen out of my pocket when I was sitting on the lumber pile"; and finally, after retrieving it from the garage, "That doesn't mean I failed, it just means I need improvement."

Mrs. Reilly, the principal, summoned my parents to the school, and then they sat me down and told me what I dreaded to hear more than anything: "You have to repeat the sixth grade."

Left back. Left back! How could I ever look any of my friends in the face again? They tried to comfort me. "You've always been the youngest and smallest in your class, and now you'll be with kids more your own age," my father said. "You'll make new friends," my mother added. "You'll have already done the work, so it will be easier the second time around."

That night, my mother came into my room and sat on the edge of my bed, brushed the hair from my forehead, damp from a tear-soaked pillow. "You'll get over it," she said.

And I did.

Miss Gold – my sixth-grade teacher the second time around – had taken over the class at P.S. 8 late in the fall of 1960, just after the sudden departure of Mrs. McCarthy. The explanation at the time, at least around the schoolyard, was that the latter teacher had "flipped out," but that was not exactly the case. Her mental problems were more probably deep-rooted.

Mrs. McCarthy had a thing about wasting paper. She encouraged her students to write on both sides of their composition sheets and to save pieces of paper with blank sides for "scrap." But as the school year progressed, desks began to bulge with the hoarded scrap paper. Our teacher began to insist that papers with even a few square inches of blank space be saved for future use. By November, she refused to allow anything to be put in the waste cans, not even used tissues. Eraser crumbs and pencil shavings had good second uses, she insisted. Her classroom became a recycling nightmare.

Mrs. McCarthy had a thick head of hair, wavy and dyed red. She would often sit for minutes at a time at her desk, her furrowed brow resting in one palm while the other hand massaged the nape of her neck as we sat silently, awaiting instructions. Then she would suddenly leap to her feet and begin to accuse us of secretly using other waste cans in the building to dispose of perfectly good paper, and of conspiring against her. That's when the school board stepped in.

It did not take Miss Gold long to figure out that Mrs. McCarthy's madness might have been hastened by her pupils. She found them to be spoiled, unruly and incorrigible, but that made them no different than any other sixth-graders. What bothered her most was an eerie sense that these students were much worse; that what flowed in her classroom was an undercurrent of cruelty.

Almost from that first day in late November when she had taken over the sixth-grade class, Miss Gold had begun to suspect that her predecessor's mental affliction had been worsened by the behavior of her students, that it was likely they had baited her, deliberately provoked her to fits of rage just for the theatrical thrill of it. She was beginning to realize how cruel children can be. A sickening feeling came over her when she witnessed the way her students treated Katrina.

Pretty and a little plump, Katrina had long blond hair that she frequently wore in two braids. She almost never smiled and rarely looked up from her book, or her desk, or her feet. She seldom spoke, and when she did her words were barely audible. She would have gone unnoticed and unheard if not for her German accent.

Katrina was the target of merciless teasing. She could not utter a complete sentence without inciting a chorus of giggles. Boys would follow her down the hall, goose-stepping like Nazi soldiers. They would click their heels and say "Heil, Hitler!" all the time. She was excluded from all games and conversations. Her classmates shunned her.

What worried Miss Gold the most was the hate she sometimes perceived. It was not obvious, more like a chilling draft from a mysterious source. Did these students inherit animosity for a former enemy from their parents, many who fought against the Germans not so long ago? Although the war had been over for 15 years, Adolf Eichmann, the "architect of the Holocaust," had only recently been captured in Argentina by Israeli agents.

One day, just before Christmas vacation, Katrina was ill and did not come to school. Miss Goldstein took the opportunity to scold the class, and she did so vehemently and passionately. The effect was that the children felt mortified and deservedly embarrassed by their behavior.

Some of her classmates made promises to themselves to be especially kind to Katrina when she returned, but the child did not come to school the next day, nor the next. Then the long Christmas break arrived, and when they came back to P.S. 8 in January, Katrina wasn't there. Her father had been transferred to a job in another city, and the family had moved.

"I hope you're all very satisfied with yourselves," Miss Gold said. I hope you're very happy with how cruelly you treated that little girl."

Her stinging sarcasm was not necessary. The wound had been inflicted, and there was now no chance it would heal.

I still think about Katrina and am haunted by the desperate sadness that I imagine was in her eyes, and by regret and my own guilt about the misery heaped upon her.

The main building of Public School No. 8 was built in 1896, a fortress of steel and stone and brick. The long halls, smelling of milk, floor wax, vomit and sweeping compound, were lined with tall, windowless doors and transoms. I remember most the gymnasium/ cafeteria.

When the weather was nice, we had our gym class on the playground or ran wind sprints on the street at the rear entrance to the school. But in winter and on rainy days we were in the gym, performing exercises that no school district would ever allow now. I imagine that after so many ruptured spleens and broken arms, someone probably decided that forcing grade-school children to perform on the pommel horse and parallel bars was maybe not such a good idea. Ditto for climbing the rope to the top of the gym and slapping the girder to which it was attached. I get a knot in my groin just thinking about that now.

The girls dreaded gym class the most, and it's no wonder. They were required to wear gym suits: clownish white costumes that billowed at the hips; that, and also to be humiliated in relay races and dodge ball.

Every so often, there would be a dance in the gym – a sock hop, our parents called it, even though they didn't make us take off our street shoes to protect the gym floor. Girls had to wear party dresses, and boys were required to wear sport coats and ties. I was peculiarly fashion-conscious for an 11-year-old, and my idea of looking cool included white athletic socks. My parents refused to allow me to leave the house dressed up as I was in anything but black socks, so I had to hide my while socks in my pockets and change into them on my way to the dance.

Dancing with girls was exciting, although I was a little too young and a little to dense to understand why. My mother had forced me to take dancing lessons at Mr. Barclay's School of Dance, so I could do a mean fox trot and cha-cha. But I preferred the slow box step, to the sound of the Fleetwoods singing "Mr. Blue," when I could touch the crinkly material around a girl's waist and feel her soft, damp hand within mine, and smell her shampooed hair and wonder why all of that seemed suddenly so interesting.

My long newspaper career had its start back in 1960, when I signed on as a carrier for the Herald-Statesman, Yonkers' daily afternoon paper. I'd pedal over to Ellison Avenue after school, pick up my bundle, fold my papers into "tomahawks," and load them in the twin baskets straddling my rear wheel. Then I'd fly down the sidewalk, flinging the folded papers at the front doors of my customers. A perfectly thrown tomahawk would smack against the door waist-high, then fall open, front-page up, on the doormat.

The money was good, for 1960. With tips, my profit was usually $7 a week. Combined with my 50-cent-a-week allowance, I had all the money a boy could need for Mad Magazines, baseball cards, punk, ammo for my pea shooter, caps, rubber spiders, Top Cat figurines, comic books, decals, Hostess cupcakes, bottles of 7-Up, yo-yos, handlebar streamers, spaldeens (those pink balls we used for stickball), balsawood gliders, candy bars, model cars and glue.

The job also made it possible to indulge in some of the luxuries available in Bronxville Proper: banana splits at the ice cream parlor, bowling, orange rickies at the drugstore soda counter, and the movies. For 50 cents, we could spend all of Saturday afternoon in the theater, watching cartoons, a newsreel, Three Stooges episodes and the main feature.

Life was so uncomplicated for a boy of 11, soaring free on his bicycle, when he wasn't being dragged off by his mom to dancing classes and piano lessons. But it would all get complicated soon enough.

Kids who grow up on farms know what the score is early on. They see horses acting up in the field, know how little horses are made, and figure out at a young age that people reproduce in roughly the same way.

Kids who grow up in the city, or in suburban towns like Bronxville, don't have that insight. And a kid like me, who was pretty dense to begin with, and spent much of his time and mental activity in his own dream world, was pretty much clueless about sex. At 11, I honestly thought that women became pregnant automatically when they reached a certain age or situation in life. I was vaguely aware of sex but thought it was just unnatural, filthy shenanigans engaged in by criminally-minded teenagers.

I liked girls and had liked them from earliest memory. By age 11, we were going to boy-girl birthday parties and playing kissing games, but I don't think it ever occurred to me then that there could be things more pleasurable to do with girls than kissing.

Then one Saturday afternoon, one of my classmates and I rode our bikes north of town to the abandoned villa. Up a steep hill overgrown with wild rose and sumac was a house long ago given up to the elements. It had been a sprawling, two-story house with white stucco walls and a red tile roof. All the windows had been broken; saplings grew from the gutters, the floors were covered with broken glass and leaves and gravel that had once been mosaic tiles. We loved to walk through these ruins and imagine what life had been like there so many years earlier.

But we were not alone that day. When we came up through the jungle, we saw a couple of girls, sitting on the concrete railing on the portico, sharing a cigarette. We tried to ignore them, but one of them yelled, "Hey, you, c'mer!" We did not recognize them. They were not from our school and looked a little older. They must have been from Tuckahoe.

We traded the usual insults and my friend and I turned away from them to do our exploring. But they followed us. We split up, and they split and followed us still. I was not comfortable. Had these been boys, they would have been picking a fight. The girl following me was acting tough, but she was not looking to fight. She was teasing me, telling me what goofy looking hair I had, what ugly sneakers. And then she said, "I bet you'd like to feel me up."

I screwed up my face as if I'd just smelled a dead animal. "No!" I said. "Who'd want to touch you?"

"Well, I wouldn't let you anyway," she said.

A little later, the other girl said she had to get home and they left, and my friend and I walked around the back of the house, not saying much. Those girls were gone, but something heavy, like dread, still hung in the air. I didn't understand what had happened that day, why I had felt anxious and afraid and angry and excited. Only later would I realize that my dream world had started to crumble.

I go back to Millard Avenue almost every day. Not physically, of course, because it is 400 miles away. I go back there in my imagination because it is the street of my youth.

All of my big ideas – the good ones and the silly ones – seem to start on the pavement of that wide and shady boulevard and to sprint down the middle of it before sprouting wings and taking flight.

My family lived on Millard Avenue from 1958 to 1962, just enough time for a youngster to collect enough vivid images to last him a lifetime.

ALL DRESSED FOR CHURCH IN SPRING 1959, BY
THE DOGWOOD IN FRONT OF THE HOUSE AT 142
MILLARD AVENUE.

Ours was the house where 500 tulips and two huge dogwoods bloomed in the spring, the house covered with roses in summer. Ours was the yard in which kids played Red Light, Green Light until past dusk.

On Millard Avenue, right in front of our house, was home plate: a manhole cover with iron lettering in a semi-circle that read, "CITY OF YONKERS." The next manhole cover, up the street toward town, was second base. We marked first and third on the curbstones with chalk, and that was our stickball field.

"Car coming!" someone would tell, and we would stop the game and move out of the way.

I can see so clearly in my memory even the flotsam along the curbs and at the storm grates: acorns, Good Humor wrappers and sticks, bits and pieces of exploded firecrackers, the seed pods of maple trees.

Sometime after the incident at the abandoned villa, I sat on the curb on Millard Avenue one summer afternoon, contemplating the debris between my sneakers. Here was a mortified and miserable 11-year-old boy who had just pieced together the mysteries of life. Now that I knew how babies were made, finally, how could I ever face my parents again? How could I ever look into their faces without thinking of their disgusting and shameful behavior?

I walked up and down the street, cut across the field, crossed the spiked bridge over the creek and into the meadow, alone. Somehow, in the heat of that awful day, I found the strength to face the facts of life, and a life made more complicated by them.

I am grown up now, to say the least, and face the miserable realities of life almost every day. I find the strength to deal with them by going back in my mind and taking that walk again.

This was my Bronxville neighborhood, and this was my street.

The street of my youth.

The thread of my life.

THE MAIN BUILDING OF TAFT SCHOOL,
JANUARY 1964.

CHAPTER TWO

Watertown

In September 1939, at the age of 13, my father was sent away to prep school, on the other side of the country, to a place he'd never been. It would be better this way, he must have been told. His father was busy dealing with communist troublemakers on his ranch in Mexico. His mother was remarried to a Navy man, and the family was hopscotching around the country, and even to Central America. With the war starting in Europe, who knew where they would be sent next.

It would be better this way, he must have told himself as he gazed from his dormitory window and considered the smoke curling from the stacks at the shoe and clothing factories in the gray town down the road. Better? He must have wondered about that, when Christmas came and he found himself in the home of a fellow student because home – wherever that was then – was just too far away.

Only in summer would he leave that place, for the bases in Panama or the Great Lakes, or California. And then in the fall he would return to his new family of 300 boys and men, sequestered in dark stone halls behind the cover of sycamores at the edge of reality, that place called Watertown.

On Sunday, Dec. 7, 1941, my father and some other boys were sitting around the radio in the living room of the headmaster's home when word came of the attack on Pearl Harbor. The war must have seemed a very distant thing from within the boundaries of the Taft School. Students were not permitted to own radios, and without regular access to newspapers, events of the war came by word of mouth as rumor.

The purpose of the school was to prepare young men for college, but the war changed that. Many graduates who might have gone on to Yale or Harvard were now headed for boot camp. Schoolwork for the class of 1944 was accelerated so that half the class - my father included - could graduate five months earlier, in January, and enter the military sooner.

My father joined the Navy, ending up with the occupying forces in Japan at the end of the war. He would return to Watertown years later for Alumni Day, taking me along with him. I remember a particular sunny Saturday afternoon in autumn, being introduced around to my dad's old buddies standing in the shade of the tent, the sound of their laughter and the clinking of ice in the highballs, the smell of limes, asking the bartender for ginger ale with a cherry, stuffing my mouth with cocktail peanuts, playing with other alumni children, one of them a strange boy with lavender eyes...

"It won't be long before you're a student here," so many people told me, squeezing my shoulder, mussing my hair. And they were right.

There is a portal to the unknown in the broom closet directly across the hall from my dormitory room. The wall to the right in the closet ends about 18 inches below the ceiling. I get on a foot stool and peer into the opening. I see daylight about eight feet away, so I jump up into the space and crawl to it. I lower myself down into space about 6 feet square, lit by a tiny, dust-caked window. It is a dead space created many years ago when rooms and walls were rearranged in this gloomy five-story building. It is a secret place, known only to me...

I visit this place in my dreams every so often. But my time in that dormitory was so long ago that I do not know if that space actually existed or if it was always an invention of my mind.

How long ago? Let me tell you. John Kennedy was our president. No one in this country had ever heard of the Beatles. The cool guys wore skin-tight chinos and white, woolen athletic socks and penny loafers and Madras sport jackets. On the phonograph in the recreation room, we played our Bobby Vee and Ventures LPs and tried to decipher the slurred smutty lyrics of "Louie, Louie." Color television was still a novelty, but TV sets, and even radios, were not allowed at school anyway.

Our only exposure to the outside world came from the newspapers and magazines we bought in Watertown on Saturday afternoons. But my classmates and I, 14 years old and free of our parents for the first time, were not much interested in news of the outside world. We were too busy trying to survive in this petri dish of peer pressure that was our school. We had no time to worry about the world of adults. Our planet was our school, in the universe of Connecticut. And then everything changed on November 22, 1963.

In the weight room, steamy and smelling of sweat, someone shouted, "The president's been shot!"

I had just hoisted a bar to my collarbone. I lowered it to my thighs, then let it go with a clang. I felt dizzy and dropped to my knees. Everyone else ran out of the room.

The news came to us through the day from some of the

upperclassmen who had been watching television in the masters' apartments. On the way to dinner, I heard one boy say, "This is an ideal time for the Russians to attack." I wondered if we would be told to crouch under our desks, as we had in grade school, or whether they would herd us into the basement.

Four hundred boys eating a meal in a single hall was normally a noisy affair, but that Friday night was eerily quiet - just the clinking of glasses and silverware and the hiss of whispers. It would have been an unusual meal, the last before Thanksgiving break, even if nothing monumental had happened that day, because it was to be a "sacrifice meal" of soup, crackers, bread and water. It was an annual observance planned by students; the money not spent on food from that dinner would be donated to feed the poor.

My mother had fixed all my favorite dishes for my first visit home, but no one was much interested in food, and our conversation seemed trivial and unimportant. We spent the weekend glued to the TV, like everyone else in America.

When we returned to school a week later, everything looked different, although nothing had physically changed. Of course, it was us who had been changed, just as my father had been changed that Sunday afternoon 22 years earlier.

The pond between the old school building and the new science building was frozen over when we returned from Christmas break, and it snowed heavily our first night back. My roommate insisted on sleeping with the window open, no matter how cold it got. I wore socks and a woolen sweater to bed and still lay there shivering, part from the cold, part from anxiety.

My evenings were spent in study hall,
hunched over one of a hundred ancient,
oaken desks lined in military file under
the stern gaze of the prefect.

I prayed that there would be no nuclear war or more snipers shooting presidents, and I dreaded the morning and what it would bring: Latin, American literature, French, algebra. I had struggled from the first week of classes with the same problems that had dogged me through grade school. I tried hard to focus on what my teachers were saying, but always, after a few minutes, their voices trailed off and I would mentally exit the room, soaring off to more exciting places, leaving the boy, seemingly awake, blinking, mouth agape, behind.

You really have to try harder, my parents told me during break. You have no idea how proud your father is that you're at Taft now, my mother said. Please don't disappoint him. I won't, I won't, I said.

But I fell behind in every class. My teachers - they were called masters there - did not ride my case; instead, they ignored me. The bright students received the attention; I was invisible.

The gray days of January ticked slowly away, my afternoons spent on the wrestling mats, wet with sweat, my evenings in study hall, hunched over one of a hundred ancient, oaken desks lined in military file, under the stern gaze of the prefect.

As many other boys did, I mailed my dirty clothes home in a laundry box - a black cardboard suitcase bound with cloth straps. My mother would launder the clothes and mail them back to me, usually with some sort of treat tucked in: packages of Oreos or Keebler's Pecan Sandies. After mail call one day, I hauled the box back to my room and opened it to find not cookies but something else quite different. My heart raced. Euphoria! Suddenly, everything was right with the world. I wasn't going to be invisible anymore.

You have to understand that we were not permitted to have radios at school. The administration considered them a distraction from our studies. We weren't allowed to have record players in our dorm rooms, either, but there were record players in the recreation rooms in each of the dormitories. Needless to say, popular music was slow getting to us.

At the end of Christmas break, there was a great buzz about this new group from England, and some boys had heard one of the group's songs on the radio before returning to school. Sure, some boys had transistor radios hidden in their rooms and put them to their ears in bed at night to hear the crackling signal of WABC from New York, with Bruce Morrow - "Cousin Brucie" - playing the new single by the Beatles. Word of them was starting to hum around school, and then I received my laundry box.

My mother had bought me the 45 rpm of "I Want to Hold Your Hand." I picked it out of the box and regarded it in disbelief. It hadn't reached the record store in Watertown yet. No one on my floor had this record. I might be the only one in my dormitory, or even the whole school who had this record.

I flew up the stairs to the fifth-floor rec room, put it on the spindle and cranked the volume all the way up. I opened the windows. Kids started to wander in the room to listen. We passed the record sleeve around. Cool guys, upperclassmen who would have never acknowledged my existence, asked who owned the record, then asked me how I got it. I said I had connections. (How could I tell them that my mommy bought it for me?)

For a few days, I was popular. I wouldn't lend the record to anyone, but I'd go and play it for them. Of course, my time in the limelight was brief. Soon lots of people had that 45, and then "She Loves You," and then the album, "Meet the Beatles." But there was an excitement about the Beatles that was afflicting the student body, and I was part of that. We stopped cutting our hair, and we started rebelling against the masters who insisted we cut it.

Just as the assassination had changed us, so had this music. Sure, we would still listen to the Beach Boys, but we had this sense now that we were riding a wave, leaving our old lives behind.

Turning 15, I experienced a growth spurt, both physically and mentally. The cuffs of my pants were suddenly three inches above my ankles, and the additional height gave me a different vantage point to view the adults around me.

Adults had let us down; they had screwed up the world. We seemed to be close to nuclear annihilation, our president had been assassinated, we were breathing filthy air, and our "advisers" in Vietnam were doing much more than advising. It was time for young people to take control, and we would do it to Beatles' music.

Defiance came in baby steps. A day student invited me to his home in Watertown for a weekend, and we walked around town smoking Salems and pestering girls he knew from grade school. I fell for one of them, Joan, the daughter of a hardware-store owner, and a few weeks later I sneaked her up to my dorm room for a look-around one Saturday afternoon while everyone else was up the hill watching our hockey team play.

In American Lit, I was tired of being invisible. The master read the last sentence of Chapter 9 of "The Red Badge of Courage": "The red sun was pasted in the sky like a wafer." He said the wafer was a religious symbol, the body of Christ. I argued that maybe Stephen Crane was just trying to describe exactly how the sun looked, and that it was no symbol. (I remembered, in my days as an altar boy, the perfect circles of paper-thin wafers lying in the silver dish...)

The master glared at me. "The Tall Soldier, was his name not 'Jim Conklin'?" he shouted, spittle flying from his lip. "Jim Conklin, the initials J and C, as in Jesus and Christ, as in the Lord's march up Calvary! Is this beginning to penetrate your thick skull yet?"

Well, maybe he had a point, but I wasn't going to acknowledge it. I shrugged and smirked, which made him even angrier. "You see me after class," he said, not addressing me by name because he had no idea what it was. My grades were already perilously low, and this certainly wouldn't help. But I felt a twinge of satisfaction, of pride at not going down without a fight.

Aside from being dumber than most of my classmates, there were other curious differences. Many of these boys were rich, and rich people are strange, I discovered.

Not that I - or my father - were not also privileged, our families able to afford tuition at a private school. But these boys were pedigreed, and I was more of a mutt. My father had married a Polish girl from New Haven, whom he met while he was at Taft. My mother used to say she was from the other side of the tracks, that her family was so poor that they didn't know where their next meal was coming from, although that was an exaggeration. But through her I maintained a connection to a world to which my rich classmates were oblivious.

Our school arranged a dance with a nearby finishing school for girls. They were a different species than the girls I had know, than the girls at the high school in Watertown. "Do you sail?" one would ask as we swayed on the dance floor. "Where does your family summer?" another would query. I had no idea what the verb "to summer" meant.

Many of my classmates had answers to these questions, rattling off their yacht-racing victories, listing their favorite haunts in the Hamptons.

My roommate, Scott, invited me to his home in Greenwich, Conn., for a few days over Easter break. I think I liked Scott because he was as dumb as I was. But he was, well, odd. He had terrible acne, and the way he dealt with it was to shave very close with a sharp razor, lopping off the tops of all his pimples, blotting his bleeding face with a towel, then generously splashing his face with shaving lotion. He'd then lie on his bed and muffle his screams with his gory pillow.

All in Scott's family were sailors who seemed to spend their time commuting between yacht club and country club. My first night at his house, Scott told me we had to dress for dinner. "Where are we going?" I asked. Nowhere, he told me. He said his family always dressed for dinner at home, that it was his father's rule that you had to wear a coat and tie to sit at the table.

"Do you have a tie I can borrow?" I asked him. He fingered through a few on the rack in his closet. "Here, take this one," he said. "It doesn't seem to have too much blood on it."

The school restricted students from returning home on weekends and discouraged visits from parents except for specific occasions, like Mothers' Visiting Day in late April. I had written to my mother that it was not necessary for her to come all the way to Watertown, but she insisted.

On that Saturday afternoon, I waited for her at my dorm room window. I was hoping to catch site of the white Buick convertible as in pulled into the circle so that I could rush down and head her off before she came into the building and everyone saw her. But she must have parked somewhere else, because all of a sudden I saw her walking - almost wobbling - toward the main door, where everyone could see her in her white hat and white gloves and her navy-blue maternity suit, clutching a gray leather purse above her protruding abdomen, "ready to drop one," as I was sure some of my classmates might snigger.

I flew down the steps and caught her just outside the main doors. She hugged me, right out there in the open, and my cheeks burned. I steered her in the direction from which she'd come. "I'll give you a tour," I told her. "Let's go see the hockey rink."

"Hockey? It's nearly May," she said, but she took my arm and up the hill we went.

We talked awhile about my younger sisters, then we were silent. A smile began to take over her expression.

"You're embarrassed because I'm pregnant."

I stammered and tried to deny it.

"That's all right, I understand," she said. "I'm a little embarrassed myself. Almost 38 years old. I'll be an old lady in the hospital with all those young mothers. But maybe you should feel proud that your mother's young enough to be expecting."

That was little comfort.

"This walking wears me out," she said. "Why don't we just drive into town for something to eat."

I thought about all the other boys with their older and unpregnant mothers crowding the restaurant in Watertown. She must have read my mind.

"Well, maybe we can go to Waterbury instead. We won't have as much trouble getting a table there."

She could sense my relief. She laughed and gripped my arm tighter, and my thoughts turned from the horror of humiliation to hamburgers and fresh fries.

MY FATHER CAME FOR VISITING DAY IN
MAY 1964.

How do we revisit our most painful memories? Sometimes it's easiest to detach, to be an objective observer, omnipresent, examining ourselves from a distance. And so I see a boy, standing beside his father in the shade of the new leaves that have sprouted on a giant oak. It is early May and Father's Visiting Day. The boy has grown almost six inches since September and now is almost as tall as his dad. They stroll across the lawn, the man kneading the muscles in his son's shoulder as they go.

The boy is animated, describing his experiences at track, now his favorite sport. He has made the junior varsity team, running sprints and hurdles. He loves the sport because there is so little to learn, so little to think about. There are few rules and even less strategy to learn in running a 100-yard dash. You just run. To do better, run faster. That's all.

The boy leads his father up the hill to the track, to the sawdust pits for the pole vault and high jump, the circles for discus and the hammer. They are alone in the breeze, and the black gravel crunches beneath their shoes.

The boy rattles on about meets and races, but his father wants to talk about grades. The last marks had been bad. Are you going to be able to pull these grades up? Will you be able to pass? His father wants to know. The boy needs to offer some assurance, some hope, but the words don't come. Tears well in his eyes, then run down his cheeks. He wipes his face with the sleeve of his coat and tries to answer, but all that comes out is a deep sob, and his father, awkwardly, puts both his arms around him.

I tried, I really did, the boy finally manages. But the work is too hard, and everyone else is so smart, and nothing I do is ever right. Except here, on the track.

They turn and head back toward the campus, the boy offering still another promise to do better. He looks back over his shoulder at the quarter-mile oval, the bleachers baking in the sun, wondering if by some miracle he might be able to run there again next spring.

My brother was born at the end of May, but it was a difficult birth and my mother was still in the hospital when my father picked me up at school for summer break. We stopped at the hospital on our way home. I pulled a chair up to her bedside. She made one of those comical fake frowns and pushed my hair back.

"You have such a nice forehead," she said. "Why do you insist on hiding it behind all that hair?"

"Oh, Mom, pompadours went out with white bucks and saddle shoes. I don't want to look like some old dweeb!"

"It's good to have you back," she said. "I wish you didn't have to go away. You'll never get to know your brother."

But staying home and going to school just down the road apparently was not an option.

The letter from Taft came a couple of weeks later. Terse and unsympathetic, it stated simply that, based on my grades, I was not invited back in the fall.

My father paled and shook with rage, but his anger was directed not at me but at the school, his school. From another room I caught bits of his telephone conversation with some administrator there. Why had they taken their sweet old time to inform him? Did they realize he was an alumnus and a contributor?

I can't think that flunking out came as a complete surprise to my parents, who by then had become accustomed to my academic struggles. But I imagine they were embarrassed. As for me, I had gone beyond the hedges of embarrassment and down the dark path of shame and humiliation. I wondered if there was something fundamentally wrong with me.

The administrator had given my father a few suggestions about prep schools that might be suitable for a boy like me, and one July morning we drove up the Taconic State Parkway into upstate New York, to the Berkshire Mountains, for a look at what I imagined was Losertown, a place where failures like me would feel right at home.

Our car's tires growled over a rutted dirt road as we approached the campus, which didn't look at all Oxfordish. Sheep grazed in pastures beyond old wooden buildings. Polished plank floors creaked beneath our shoes. Maple trees shook and bent, turned the pale sides of their leaves up and beat them against the windows in the whistling wind as we waited for the interviewer. I scanned the playing fields on a vast plateau overlooking the blue-green valley: baseball diamonds, clay courts, goal posts, soccer nets.

No track.

It is September 1964, and I am marching in a long line of boys that winds around a pond and into what looks like a big red barn. It is actually the chapel, I overhear, and as we file in we take seats in long, spindled wooden benches. Our parents, meanwhile, are trudging up stairs and filling seats in balconies to each side and behind us. The chapel is a cacophony of chair legs screeching on wooden planks, creaking floorboards, throat clearing and respectful whispers. Mothers fan themselves with programs. I look up and see in the framework of massive beams a pair of sparrows flying as fast as shooting stars.

The headmaster takes the podium and, acknowledging that many of us are new to this place, explains that these buildings were constructed by the Shakers in the previous century, and that because the Shakers were celibate, they no longer exist. Although the school is nondenominational, he explains, it embraces some of the spiritual strengths of the Shakers, and that the school's motto is "Hands to Work, Hearts to God."

I begin to wonder if I've just enrolled in a monastery.

This building in which you sit was not a barn, not a chapel, but a tannery, he explains. The Shakers hung their chairs on pegs and did their wild and crazy dancing in some other building. This building is a monument to the self-sufficiency of the people who came before us, he drones on.

Pssst! I hear from behind me. Pssst! Hey Taftee! somebody is whispering. I turn around and am shocked to see Tim, a boy from the third floor of my dorm at Taft, a fellow nerd, someone who shared cigarettes with me on walks through downtown Watertown. I turn back and stare at the headmaster's moving mouth. What's Tim doing here? I think.

I turn around again and give him a quizzical look. He shrugs, flicks his eyebrows, tells me "Me too" silently.

So, I'm not the only loser to be uninvited back. When we file out of the chapel, I catch up with him and he rattles off the names of four or five other classmates that have also flunked out, including my odd, zit-shaving roommate, Scott.

Suddenly, I feel less lonely.

Like Boy Scout Camp, and like Taft, Darrow School had its traditions and rituals regarding "new boys." We'd been warned about doors we weren't to use, tables not to sit at, the proper way of addressing older students, that sort of thing. There were a lot of rules;

it was easy to forget one. And so I found myself one evening in my first week at my new school sitting on the floor of my room in Ann Lee Cottage with a shoeshine kit beside 30 pairs of scuffed shoes piled in a pyramid. One of the seniors stood in my doorway, shirtless, arms folded, grinning with satisfaction. "When you're finished, be sure to put them back in their proper closets," he said.

"How do I know which closets they go in... Sir?"

He laughed. "You'll figure it out."

From time to time through the night, upperclassmen would walk by my door, look in and make some sort of smart comment. This was my home now, and it was grand. I was anything but invisible here.

Darrow had less than half the students as Taft. They told me I'd know everyone's name by Thanksgiving. Everything was different. On Wednesdays we didn't even have classes. Instead, we had "Hands to Work," when everyone worked for the school. I was on the apple cider crew with six other boys. That September, we picked apples all day, which sure beat conjugating Latin verbs.

But my Taft experience haunted me. Fear of failing again churned in my guts like a bad secret. I worried about my wandering mind, wondered how I might throw a rope around it and bring it back to thinking about the homework lying in front of me in evening study hall.

It was the wandering mind that always got me in trouble, made me have to repeat sixth grade, bounced me from one home room to another in seventh, caused me to need a private tutor in eighth, and bounced me out of Taft. Would it be the same again here?

I found myself alone again, in my room, on my floor, the whole of Ann Lee Cottage completely silent save the click-bang-hiss of steam in the radiators. But this was not the same kind of solitude I had experienced that day almost a year earlier, in the weight room at Taft just after hearing that the president had been shot.

This was quite different. Everyone else was in compulsory study hall or the library, and having made high honors first term, I was permitted to study in my room.

My father was beside himself with glee. He wanted to send my grade report to the headmaster at Taft with some sort of told-you-so note. He must have thought that I was always this font of intelligence and that Taft - his alma mater - was too dumb to tap it. But my father was deluded. I was no genius; the competition at my new school wasn't as tough; through fear I had found focus; this place was too small for anyone to be invisible.

From my dorm-room window I gazed out into the night, the frosted sheep pasture across the lane was gray-blue in starlight. I could see then, beyond the silhouettes of ancient Shaker buildings and the hills dipping into the long valley beyond, that everything was going to be all right; that the world was not about to end in nuclear holocaust; that the world was still a good place in which to bring a baby, like my infant brother; that I would not stumble and fall from this new place on the mountain that was now my home.

I never regretted my days in Watertown, and whatever animosity I felt for Taft evaporated long ago. My failure there helped me become the man I am today. It taught me my limits, and how to succeed within those limits. I've had other failures since, but I've learned not to become wrapped in the humiliation but rather to cherish those experiences for the lessons they teach.

We all have depths of the soul to which we must descend from time to time. We all have our own Watertowns.

CHAPTER THREE

The Spirits of Lebanon

I've often written about Darrow, the boarding school where I spent three years in the 1960s. Its history is odd and fascinating; the school itself is a National Historic Landmark, with many of its building comprising the first Shaker community in the U.S. The Shakers, more formally known as the United Society of Believers in Christ's Second Coming, once numbered 6,000 members living in 18 major communities in eight states. But because they were celibate and gained new members only by conversion and adoption, the sect largely died out by the early 20th century, and now only a handful remain in the community at Sabbathday Lake, Maine.

We teenage boys cloistered there in those days of the middle of the last century treated our school's Shaker heritage like an embarrassing family secret. The idea of celibacy was incomprehensible; we were obsessed with losing our virginity, not preserving it. We did our best to ignore the history, but we could not escape it. The Shakers first came to that Berkshire mountainside near New Lebanon in 1781, and 100 years later had built Utopia. Then they dwindled, disappeared. We felt the chill of their presence in the dark corners of old buildings, imagined their whispers in the damp woods.

"The Shakers selected this spot for a purpose," wrote Cheryl Moore, an art teacher and theater director, on Darrow's Web site.

THE LAFLIN WHITEHEAD CHAPEL ON THE
CAMPUS OF THE DARROW SCHOOL IN NEW
LEBANON, N.Y., IS BETTER KNOWN AS THE
TANNERY, FOR WHICH IT WAS USED BY THE
SHAKERS WHO BUILT IT IN 1834.

"Something intangible happens to you here. You see poppies in bloom that were originally planted by the Shakers 200 years ago, and you feel a tremendous connection."

I'm wondering, now that a number of my own classmates have died, if someday, perhaps even now, the students at Darrow feel the chilling presence of not just the Shakers but the students of long ago. That place has been worn smooth by humanity; it is rich in experience; its stories need to be told.

The poet Robert Frost taught my roommate Dean and I how to bend birches. We read "Birches" in class, and then one Sunday afternoon in late September went up into the woods behind the school to do it.

> *"...He learned all there was*
> *To learn about not launching out too soon*
> *And so not carrying the tree away*
> *Clear to the ground. He always kept his poise*
> *To the top branches, climbing carefully*
> *With the same pains you use to fill a cup*
> *Up to the brim, and even above the brim.*
> *Then he flung outward, feet first, with a swish,*
> *Kicking his way down through the air to the ground..."*

Up the side of the mountain we went, bending the white-barked trees as we went, until we reached a pit, sparkling at the bottom, bits of sunlight bouncing off broken bottles. We went down to investigate.

It was an old dump, ancient really. A recent rain had washed the soil from the top of the pile, from which protruded old medicine bottles, some of them cobalt blue, some with the corks still in them. We kicked through the pile. Here was the rusted business end of a pitchfork. Here a spring and a lead pipe. Then I pulled out a boot, much of it gone but the sole intact. It was an old boot for sure. We surmised it could have belonged to one of the Shakers. I brushed the dirt off and examined it: a hole clear through beneath the ball of the foot, the heel worn away on one side.

Even at that age, I was a skeptic, never having believed in ghosts or anything paranormal. But holding that shoe gave me a chill. Although its owner was probably long dead, this thing still spoke for him, still told me about his gait and the way he dragged his heel.

Would I leave these marks of my existence here? I thought about the wooden benches we sat in for the vespers service every night, the depressions, smooth as a baby's skin, worn into the wood first by the rumps of Shakers and then by generations of schoolboys in corduroy pants. These material things long outlive us, but our use of them transforms them and lends them our spirit. Then I looked at the young birches, bowing respectfully toward the ground from our play, and wondered if they'd straighten or just grow the way we'd bent them.

Dean threw himself away from the thin trunk and was lowered slowly to the ground, collapsing in laughter and a shower of yellowing leaves. Pieces of poem tumbled from his lips.

"One could do worse than be a swinger of birches!" he yelled.

Our school was isolated from the rest of the world. The building lined a dirt road that came up from the village of New Lebanon, wound up through the woods and across the state line, where it met up with Route 20, the main road for traffic to Pittsfield, Mass. Almost no one used this old Shaker road, and the upper part was rocky and deeply rutted. But every so often, a carload of teenagers would pass through the campus, yelling insults and obscenities and hurling empty beer cans from their windows.

One afternoon, a car filled with boys came roaring down the road in a cloud of dust and slowed as it passed a group coming back from the gym. "Darrow fairies!" someone yelled. The group quickly surmised that they were Pittsfield boys headed down to the village in New York state to buy beer. (The drinking age was 18 in New York then, and 21 in Massachusetts.) Word spread quickly that the car might be coming back through campus. When it did, 60 or 70 "Darrow fairies" streamed out of their dormitories, screaming at the top of their lungs and waving baseball bats and lacrosse sticks. I was up the road in front of my dorm, Ann Lee Cottage, and watched the road fill with students and saw the car come to a sliding stop, then move rapidly in reverse, fishtailing back toward the valley.

Another time, on a warm, spring Sunday afternoon, a convertible came down the road, a teenage girl standing on the back seat with nothing on from the waist up. I was elsewhere when this happened, much to my disappointment. I peppered the witnesses with questions: "Who else was in the car? Did she say anything? How slow was the car going? Did you get a good look? Was she good-looking?"

On warm spring nights when no wind was blowing up from the valley and we had the windows at Ann Lee propped wide open, you could hear some of the traffic on Route 20. One night, just after lights out, we heard a crash – the sounds of snapping trees and twisting metal, and then an explosion – and then a wash of yellow light came through the back windows. We ran out the back door and beheld what was left of a fireball in the sky, now pierced by a tower of flames.

A few days later, we hiked up to the scorched scar in the woods. It had been a gasoline tanker, we were told. The driver had died. There was almost nothing left of the truck. The aluminum tank had melted and flowed like lava and hardened into rivulets that we snapped off and kept as souvenirs. This was near the old dump we had found. I imagined the aluminum flowing down into the pit and filling the old Shaker boot, creating a sculpted foot of the owner that might last for millennia. What would future archaeologists think?

The world intruded on us with violence and lust and fire and death on the mountain. We were isolated and protected, but we yearned for the world. We were well cared for, but we never stopped plotting our escape.

"Tannery Pond Concerts presents a season of six to seven chamber concerts between May and October in the Tannery on the grounds of the Darrow School in New Lebanon, NY.

"The Tannery, built by the Shakers in 1834, is a plain barn-like structure of warmly resonant wood unusually favorable to the sounds of chamber music, whether string ensemble, voice, piano, or small orchestra. Its size (it seats 290) fosters an intimate and interactive relationship between performers and artists, providing an unusual and exciting opportunity for closeness with the renowned artists that have appeared at Tannery Pond since its inception in 1991."

I stumbled upon the Tannery Pond Concerts Web site by accident. It got me to thinking. I guess musicians from all over the world are performing in the old tannery now. It was formally known on campus at the Laflin Whitehead Chapel, and we knew it well. It was where the entire school assembled every night but Saturday for vespers, a contemplative service before supper, and for church on Sunday.

I like to imagine that some of the richness of the acoustics of that building is due to the history of sound produced within it. I like to think that its oak and chestnut beams and woodwork have absorbed a couple of centuries of sound that are teased out by the vibrations from oboe and viola.

What sounds? How about the low rumble of 175 boys entering at the north door, descending the steps to the cellar, kicking off their muddy rubber boots, then ascending the steps at the south end and marching into the chapel. Or picture the suppressed laughter of a row of boys reacting to an inadvertent fart. The droning voices of a student body singing Shaker hymns under duress. The squawking of ducks copulating on Tannery Pond. The creaking of cherry benches. The chirping and fluttering of birds in the rafters. The low buzz of a June bug, tapping against dusty balcony windows. The groaning of timbers leaned on by wind. The sharp, scolding lecture of a headmaster railing against ungentlemanly conduct.

Have these sounds escaped into space, or are they trapped in the old barn forever?

I have gone back to that place. The last time, in 1997, my roommate Dean and I sat alone there for awhile, in the afternoon, the chapel on fire with the light of the descending sun, not saying anything. Just listening. Just listening to the spirits.

Without television or radio, our access to the outside world was limited to the U.S. mail, the copy of the daily newspaper available in the library and the three pay telephones in the basement of Wickersham Hall. We relied on our masters – that's what we called the

MY ROOMMATE, DEAN HALL, TOOK THIS
PHOTO OF ME STANDING BY CHERRY LANE,
WHICH WAS NOT FAR FROM OUR DORMITORY.
IT WAS A DIRT ROAD THAT EVENTUALLY
DISAPPEARED IN DEEP WOOD AND WAS A
FAVORITE PLACE TO HIKE AND BEND BIRCHES.

teachers, who also lived at the school and had televisions in their living quarters – to inform us. But we did have opportunities to escape this shelter.

Traveling to other boys' schools for games, or to girls' schools for dances, wasn't really getting out in the world, however. We were just moving from one shelter to another. Still, the dances were exciting and an opportunity for mischief.

I can recall a winter night in Albany, slow-dancing to Simon & Garfunkel's "Sounds of Silence," in the darkened rec hall at St. Agnes Academy for Girls, chaperones patrolling like prison guards. We were damp with sweat and desire, breathing through perfumed hair. Thigh to thigh we danced, and then later a bunch of us sneaked out the door to huddle in the cold dark to share a forbidden cigarette.

There were times, when traveling to and from school from home, that we were loose in the world. They took a busload of us from school to the Albany train station just before Thanksgiving 1965. We were all dressed for travel in coats and sport jackets and London Fog trench coats, most of us headed for New York City, and from there to home. I went straight to a kiosk in the station and bought a pack of cigarettes. Soon I'd be on the train, in the bar car and trying out my new fake ID and being served gin and tonics. I was feeling grown-up, but I was only 16 and uncommonly naïve. I'd always been that way – the last kid on the block to believe in Santa Claus, the last kids to realize how babies were made. I was so trusting of adults and sure they would never lie to kids or engage in filthy physical activity.

While sitting and smoking in the waiting area, a man about twice my age approached me. "I'm in a bit of a fix," he said. "I need some help. Are you interested in earning $20?"

"Sure!" I blurted out. "But I've got to catch a train in an hour. What sort of work do you have?"

"It won't take long, it's just around the corner," he said.

I followed him out to the street. The sky was overcast, the same grimy gray as the streets and the dust-caked windows of buildings covered in a patina of charcoal factory soot. We walked two blocks.

"Where is this work you have?" I asked.

"My place is just around the corner," he answered.

And then I realized what was happening. I felt nauseous and fearful. "I gotta go," I said, turning and running back toward the station.

"Hey! Where are you going! It's just around the corner!" the man yelled after me, but I kept running and didn't stop until I'd found a group of my friends with which to surround myself, just in case he'd followed me back.

This clutch of three or four classmates was my shelter. Darrow may have seemed like a prison to us then, but it, and the boys that made it, was our refuge. I can understand that now.

Sister Emma Neale came to the Shaker village at New Lebanon with her mother and sister in 1853. She spent the rest of her life on the mountainside, witnessing the sect's growth, its heyday and its decline. A teacher, a weaver and maker of cloaks, a trustee of the Society of Shakers, she and her younger sister, Sarah, operated the Darrow farm into their nineties.

In 1929, when the community's numbers had dwindled, her concern turned toward the village itself. She persuaded her friend and neighbor, attorney Charles Haight, to start a school for boys that would best use the facilities of the village and preserve something of the Shaker tradition.

SISTER EMMA NEALE, WHO CAME TO
THE SHAKER VILLAGE AT NEW LEBANON
IN 1853, SAW THE ESTABLISHMENT OF
DARROW SCHOOL AS A WAY TO PRESERVE
THE TRADITIONS AND BUILDINGS OF HER
DWINDLING SECT.

Sister Emma died in 1943 at the age of 97, her sister living on a few years longer.

"Shaker" was an almost derogatory nickname for the United Society of Believers in Christ's Second Coming. In theology, the sect was similar to the Quakers, but because they believed that God would be found within the person, they were often self-absorbed during religious services and prone to dancing, mumbling and shaking. It was this behavior, and their adherence to celibacy, that often subjected them to ridicule from the outside world.

But Shaker philosophy encompassed far more than devotional practices. The following two paragraphs sum up that philosophy well. They are taken from "The Story of Darrow School," a handbook given to me in 1964 at my enrollment:

"This New Lebanon Society was not only the oldest, but the strongest, most important, and largest, of the societies. It was the model which others followed and once had 600 people, 100 buildings, and 6,000 acres of land. Almost entirely self-sustaining, the Shakers grew their food, flax, and herbs; they built their buildings, made their clothes, drugs, equipment, furniture, stoves, and tools; they provided their own dyes, lumber, waterpower, instruction, and entertainment. Shaker chairs, cloaks, and seeds were well known, for they were sold to the general public.

"As one saintly Shaker sister expressed it, 'the Shakers were thoroughly grounded in goodness.' They were celibate, they did not vote, refused to bear arms. They were a simple people – clean, prudent, temperate and resourceful. They believed in purity of mind and body, honesty and integrity in words and dealings, humanity and kindness to friend and foe, the education of children, the common ownership of property, diligence in business, manual labor, suitable employment for all, freedom from debt. They believed, too, in suitable provision being made for their people in health, sickness, and in old age."

Sister Emma had hoped these beliefs would survive as traditions at the school. What would she have thought of the Darrow School of the 1960s? What would she think of it today?

Actually, she might not be so shocked.

Darrow made it perfectly clear that it had no connection with the Shaker Society and that the school favored no particular religion. But the Shaker idea of finding God within oneself was a good fit for a non-denominational school, and the administrators made sure we had plenty of time to do that searching.

We were required to attend chapel every evening but Saturday and on Sunday morning as well. Our life at Darrow was regimental, our schedules designed to obliterate idleness. We attended classes on Saturday, too, but not on Wednesday – that was our time for "Hands to Work."

The student body was divided into work crews that spent Wednesdays doing maintenance, landscaping, repairs, farm chores and labor for Darrow Enterprises, which included the sale of apple cider, black walnut candy and wool. The designation came from the Shaker motto, "Hands to work, hearts to God." The Shakers believed that physical labor was an act of devotion, and an object made well or a job well done was in itself a prayer to the Almighty.

Often, our Wednesday chores took us over the fields and into the woods to cut brush and clear fallen timber, and we often encountered evidence there of the old Shakers and their vigorous work ethic. I am still in awe of the walls they built, of rock chiseled and tightly fit to last through centuries, and wide and flat enough to accommodate horse-drawn hay wagons. We wondered where the huge, flat stones that made the surface of this "road" had come from. And how had they gotten

The sect was informally called Shakers
because of the method of worship, in
which individuals seeking God within
themselves were prone to mumbling,
dancing and shaking.

there? It seemed as mysterious to us as the construction of the pyramids.

We resented the hard work we were made to do in those days, but inevitably some of the Shaker work ethic rubbed off and stayed with us.

Darrow has changed over the years. A few new buildings dot the campus. The student body is about 30 percent smaller, and half the students are girls now. Latin is no longer taught and there's no need for those three pay telephones in the basement of Wickersham anymore. But Wednesdays are still reserved for Hands to Work.

Sister Emma Neale would be proud.

It was possible to escape from Darrow, legally, for a weekend, if your grades and behavior were good enough. My roommate Dean invited me to his home in the fall of our senior year. But we ignored the rules and restrictions about leaving the campus, and our antics nearly got us expelled.

I couldn't remember the details of this incident, so I e-mailed Dean and asked him for his recollection.

"We were seen by the music teacher, hitchhiking (which was strictly forbidden) on Route 20 on our way to Albany and eventually my home, at that time, in Niskayuna. We had forged leave slips saying that we were going to be picked up and returned by my mother – forged in the sense that my mother didn't pick us up.

"When we returned with my mother, the headmaster questioned us (me, you, and my mother). We lied. You caved under the severe and acute stress. We were sentenced to not being allowed to leave campus for a month or so."

Dean went on to explain that we would most likely have been expelled if the headmaster had not received word that Edward McIlvain Jr., a recent Darrow graduate, had been killed in action in

Vietnam on Oct, 18, 1966.

"It seems to me we also had to put our hands to work and our hearts to God for a length of time," Dean wrote.

Yes, I do remember now working off all those penalty hours on weekends, digging a drainage ditch until we could no longer turn the frozen earth.

And now I can recall my grilling by the headmaster. He had a stern, sharply chiseled face, as if sculpted from a pine log with a tomahawk. The anger came in a rosy blush to his cheeks and forehead. I could not have known at the time that I was not the major target of that anger, or of his grief.

Looking back, I see now why we weren't kicked out of school. We had violated his trust and had been dishonest, but our headmaster could not stomach losing another two boys. Not after losing one for good.

The Shakers had built the houses in which we lived. They'd made the pegs on which we hung our clothes and cleared the fields on which we played. The inhabitants of the New Lebanon Society had died off long ago, but we lived with their spirits, surrounded by their architecture and ingenuity.

I lived in Ann Lee Cottage, named for Mother Ann, who, the Shakers believed, represented the second coming of Christ. Although it had been retrofitted with a boiler and radiators, and plumbed to add sinks, showers and toilets, it was otherwise as it was constructed in the mid 1800s. The double-hung windows (a Shaker invention) were original. Mine faced the west, and in winter, when the wind blew up from the valley, fine little piles of snow accumulated inside on the sill, and the coffee in my cup placed there the night before would be frozen solid by morning.

A SHAKER CRAFTSMAN, PHOTOGRAPHED AT
NEW LEBANON.

Handsome and utilitarian, Ann Lee Cottage was nevertheless a firetrap. Our housemaster made it quite clear what he thought about smoking, which was forbidden for all students on campus.

"I know you smoke," he would tell us, "and nothing I tell you will prevent you from doing it. But if you have to smoke, go out into the woods to do it. Because if I ever catch you smoking in this house, and putting the lives of every boy and me and my wife and children in danger, I will make sure that you are gone from this school immediately and forever."

We didn't smoke in Ann Lee Cottage.

Once, I could not contain my curiosity any longer about a third-floor closet, the door of which was painted shut. It was a long, low closet under the eaves. One Saturday afternoon, when everyone else was watching a soccer game, I worked at it with a table knife and got the door open. It was packed full of old chairs. I don't know what I expected to find, but I was disappointed.

Of course, I imagine those old Shaker chairs would now be worth a fortune today. We had no idea at the time that the old furniture we abused would someday be commanding huge sums on the auction block at Sotheby's.

Many years later, when enrollment had plummeted and the school was in poor financial shape, much of that Shaker furniture was sold. I don't think that Sister Emma Neale would have objected, though. I think she would have felt that it was not the object that is sacred, but rather the work that made it.

As far as prep schools went, Darrow was neither large nor well endowed. Often it seemed to us that we were small and poor, especially when it came to athletics. Take football, for example.

Team sports were not an option at Darrow. We couldn't field teams unless participation was mandatory. And once you had chosen your sport (in fall it was either football or soccer), you were stuck with it, and I was stuck with football.

Our equipment was substandard; the junior varsity team was still using leather helmets. And just as embarrassing were our uniforms. Although our school colors were maroon and white, our uniforms were black and orange – hand-me-downs from Princeton University.

Our coach, Harry Mahnken, had been head football coach at Princeton from 1943 until 1945, when he came to Darrow to coach football, baseball and basketball. When the Princeton team had worn out its uniforms and had gotten new ones, the Tigers' equipment manager sent the old ones to his old friend Harry.

Coach Mahnken had the visage of a man who had played football too long in a helmet without a face guard. He was a big, gruff man who revered toughness and despised foolishness. Our daily afternoon practices were hellish. Every day, he required us to conduct a brutal one-on-one drill: One player was required to stand still while the other sprinted toward him and tackled him. I seemed always to be paired with a classmate named Mike who resembled the Incredible Hulk, but with shoulder pads and without the green skin. Mike was enthusiastic about football. After sailing with me airborne for eight feet, I'd land on my back with his enormous shoulder grinding the wind out of my chest. On my hands and knees, trying to recover, I could hear Coach yelling at me, "C'mon! Get up and hit him back!"

The coach had a couple of favorite plays that bordered on foolishness. At least twice a game we'd run the double-reverse. The quarterback would take the long hike, hand off to a halfback running right, who would hand off to the other halfback running left, who

Harry Mahnken, the gruff, tough
football coach, used his connections
at Princeton University to outfit
his teams when their equipment was
destroyed in arson fires that nearly
forced the school to close.

would hand off to the receiver running right. The play was only successful if our linemen were able to stop the rush by knocking down the opponents and lying on top of them long enough for the play to be performed.

His other favorite play was a trick. The end would not join the huddle but rather trot to the sideline and pretend to be talking with the coach, although still standing on the field of play. Our team would break from the huddle and line up for a quick count. The quarterback would then find his receiver sprinting away from our coach uncovered.

My senior year on the varsity team was cut short by a bout with mononucleosis. I was never so happy to be fighting disease. I was the happiest boy in the infirmary, waking from long naps to listen to the whistles and grunts of football practice drifting through the window, hearing the HHRRRUNCH! of another victim having the wind knocked out of him by the Incredible Mike.

In a basket on our breakfast table is a book of graces my family has used for many years. One of those graces contains this sentiment: "Grant unto us a due sense of appreciation, for those whose hearts and hands have wrought for us." This was written by a Charles D. Brodhead.

I have no way of knowing for sure that this prayer was penned by the Charles D. Brodhead who was assistant headmaster at Darrow School in the 1960s, but the words "hearts and hands" sound awfully Shaker, and our Wednesday "Hands to Work" had no more enthusiastic proponent than Mr. Brodhead.

He seemed ancient to us then, but I am now as old as he was then, and I don't feel ancient at all. Charles Brodhead was a brilliant man, educated at Princeton and Oxford, and a teacher all his life. He was also a bit eccentric. We'd see him marching through the woods and up and down the lane, carrying a walking stick and wearing a tam-o'-shanter, and we'd snicker. "Crazy Charlie" is what we called him.

Even though, in our view, he was at Death's door at age 60, he was a strong and healthy man. He coached the wrestling team. He kept his big feet in hiking boots, and his big, gnarled hands were often mahogany brown with the stain of black walnuts. But it was his wild, piercing eyes that made him look a little teched.

We were in the early years of the age of individuality, of nonconformity, when people were urged to "do their own thing," yet we students were intolerant of deviation from our established standards of fashion and behavior and subjected people who were different to ridicule, and worse.

I have written here of the quaint and comical aspects of my Darrow experience; they are pleasant to remember. But there was a darker side to life on the mountain. Darrow could be a cruel place, and torturous for those who did not fit in.

In one respect, Darrow was no different than any other boarding school, or military barracks, or prison. In these places, students, soldiers or inmates engage in typical group dynamics: They establish a pecking order, recognize leaders and select victims. To avoid persecution, you had to follow the accepted norms of behavior and fashion, and it helped greatly if you were not ugly, uncoordinated, effeminate, unstable, uncool, physically disabled, or in any other way different.

Some of the nicknames boys acquired were playful, like "Ma" and "Yoyo." Other were considerably more mean-spirited: "No-Chin" and "Dogface." Worse still were the ugly slurs: "Kike," "Fag,"

THE BRILLIANT AND ECCENTRIC CHARLES
BRODHEAD.

"Queer," and "Gimp."

Boys might prey on victims for the most minor of offenses. I recall one student teased and ridiculed because his madras sport jacket was not 100 percent cotton and from Brooks Brothers but rather some cheap blended fabric from Robert Hall.

For some of us – those lucky enough to be considered cool, or at least not uncool, or perhaps just invisible – life on the mountainside was tolerable and sometimes better. For the persecuted, those were years of fear and agony, creeping from one hiding place, such as a library cubicle, to the safety of their dorm rooms.

It is only years later that the regret and shame of it all begins to seep into your consciousness. You feel awful for being part of the pack that pounced on one of these kids, or, at least, for not coming to the defense of the persecuted.

I returned for a reunion 25 years after graduation and was surprised to see that one of these victimized classmates had also shown up. Why, I wondered, would he want to resurrect such awful memories? Why would he risk ridicule again?

Perhaps going through what he did in those years at Darrow made him stronger and hardened him for life at college, and for that he was grateful.

Of course, none of us teased or ignored him at the reunion. We had grown up. We treated him as we treated our old and good friends. We pretended as if the torture never happened. But sadly, none of us had the guts to tell him, "I'm sorry."

Darrow seemed like the same place to us year after year, but the school was – and is – in a constant state of change. Students and faculty come and go, and each of them leaves an impression.

When I was a senior, many of us were thinking how wonderful it would be to try LSD. Darrow boys five years before us had no conception of mind-altering drugs; they were different from us. And the boys (and girls) who came five years after us were probably popping acid tabs for real; they were different, too.

Ned Groth, who graduated from Darrow five years before me, offered some comments on those years:

"Harry Mahnken not only was the head football coach at Princeton for a few years, he was the original coach of 150-pound football there and coached it for a dozen years or so. He helped establish the league Princeton still plays in (although they call it "sprint" football nowadays.) There's a trophy for the outstanding player at PU, the Harry A. Mahnken trophy…

"Darrow had Princeton hand-me-down football uniforms in your era because of the arson fires of 1963. Before that, Darrow had its own very nice red uniforms (check out some older yearbooks). The gym was one of the buildings torched, and all the sports equipment therein went up in smoke. In the wake of the fires, as Operation Phoenix went into action and the school fought back from the devastating loss of the (original) Dining Hall and Dairy Barn, they took whatever help they could get. Harry called on some old connections and got perfectly good year-old uniforms, if you didn't mind black and orange…

"When I was there, the Medicine Shop was unused as a school building; it was full of all kinds of Shaker 'stuff,' including a number of large machines (laundry equipment I think), dozens of seed boxes, thousands of bottles of various sizes, etc. If I only had the sense to know what to steal, it was there for the taking. All that stuff was auctioned off in 1960, when the building was starting to be renovated for use as a dorm (it opened in the fall of 1961, I think.) Richard Bethards, a beloved English teacher and frustrated actor, was the

NO ONE KNEW HOW THE MAINTENANCE
TRUCK WAS PUT INTO THE LOBBY OF THE
DAIRY BARN, OR WHO HAD COVERED IT IN
POLKA DOTS OF YELLOW PAINT.

auctioneer… I think it fetched all of about $50,000 at the time. Most of it went to local museums, like the Shaker Museum in Chatham."

When you take about 175 boys and isolate them in the Berkshire Mountains, away from television and radio and, most importantly, girls, something is going to happen. Teenage boys have a lot of energy, and when that is stifled for a long time, it builds up, finds a weak spot and explodes through it. That's how pranks happen.

In the minds of some of the seniors in the spring of 1965, that weak spot was an old panel truck used by Darrow's maintenance department. The truck, its dark blue paint faded from years of exposure to the elements, was regularly seen coughing its way up the dirt road, its gears grinding, in daily rounds to pick up trash from the dormitories. It was manned by two friendly, slow-moving and slow-witted custodians that went by the nicknames of Augie and Mon Petite, the French term of endearment that means "my little one." But Mon Petite, was anything but little. He was, in fact, huge, with a rear-end the size of a steamer trunk.

One Saturday morning, arriving for breakfast at the Dairy Barn, which was what we called the multi-purpose building that housed the gym, auditorium and dining hall, we were shocked to find the old blue truck parked in the lobby of the building, painted all over in yellow polka dots, looking like some sort of enormous, dead beetle.

How had it gotten there? The doors to the Dairy Barn were just wide enough to get it in, but how had it gotten up the flight of concrete steps? Presumably, a large number of senior boys had either carried or pushed the truck up all those steps in the middle of the night, doing it quietly enough not to waken anyone.

The entire student body was buzzing with excitement over the prank and wondering what might happen to the culprits if they were identified. The faculty did their best to appear disgusted, offended, disappointed over the outrageous offense, but they could not quite conceal their true emotions. Even with jaws tightly clenched, smiles twitched at the corners of our masters' mouths. Many of them must have thought the prank was simply brilliant.

Our headmaster delivered the obligatory lecture, but his rage lacked sincerity. No one was punished, but the seniors were ordered to restore the truck to its rightful parking spot.

The polka dots, however, were allowed to remain.

We at Darrow School in the 1960s were no more or less rebellious than teenagers anywhere. But because we could not race around in cars or get into trouble with girls, our rebelliousness was highly focused: It was all about hair. Our goal was to grow it as long as we could. The goal of our parents at home and our masters at school was to cut it.

A barber visited campus once a week. We were often ordered to get haircuts, and not doing so meant accumulating penalty hours – our leisure time reassigned to hard labor. Some boys were willing to toil in order to dodge the clippers, but it was difficult to avoid the wrath of the establishment for long. Our headmaster was so frustrated by our refusal to obey orders that he once grabbed an underclassman named Jones, dragged him into the basement of Wickersham and barbered the boy himself. A photo of the incident, taken through the basement window by a student on a dare, ended up in the yearbook.

We were not the first rebels on the mountain, or the last. Long hair now seems so harmless, especially in comparison to the contrariness of a few years earlier that resulted in the burning of buildings and nearly

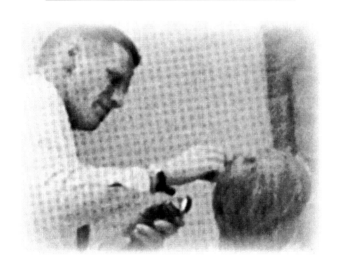

THIS PHOTO, MADE ON A DARE, SHOWS
DARROW HEADMASTER JOHN JOLINE
CUTTING THE HAIR OF A STUDENT IN THE
BASEMENT OF WICKERSHAM HALL.

the end of the school. And even some of the Shakers were dissidents. The tradition in the Shaker community was to allow males, when they reached the age of 21, to decide to stay with the community or leave for life in the world. Many of them, brought to the community as children, chose to leave, and because Shakers were celibate, the loss of these men would prove fatal to the movement. Women, apparently, had no such choice.

Young Shakers were probably no different than any young people: apt to defy their elders and surrender to their instincts. True or not, a legend persisted on the mountainside of a skeleton of an infant, wrapped in cloth, discovered hidden in a stone wall.

That legend haunted me. It was as if the anguish and the pain of that young mother had not left that place and still lingered there 100 years later. In fact, everything around me seemed to be inhabited by spirits of the past. The shaft of the shovel I used to dig ditches was smooth from the rub of hundreds of hands of students before me. The iron door latches were grooved by the countless lift of fingers. Dresser knobs forever darkened by the oil and grime of hands, door jambs dented by so many trunks and suitcases moving in and out.

In my dreams, I am transported back to the mountainside. I find myself standing on the fire escape of Ann Lee Cottage and listening to this chorus of crickets, or meandering through the creaking halls of Wickersham. I wonder if students there today might sense the wandering spirit of my dreams. I wonder if, long after I am dead, part of me will remain there, in scrapes on the floor from my chair, in notes tucked into a library book, or in a birch tree grown bent from my swinging.

CHAPTER FOUR

Life of Enos

Life was good for the Christman family in West Chester, a village just a day's journey by carriage west of Philadelphia. George, the grandson of German immigrants, had become a successful miller and millwright, and he and his wife, Sarah, had three sons who would one day follow him in the business. Then in 1843, everything changed.

When George Christman died that year, childhood ended for his eldest son, Enos, not yet 15 years old. While still attending public school, Enos found work as a clerk and did farm chores to help support his widowed mother and younger brothers. That being not enough, a year later he was bound into a five-year apprenticeship at the West Chester Record to learn the printing trade under the supervision of its editor, Henry Evans.

The position was a fortunate opportunity for the Christman family, made possible when apprentice Bayard Taylor left the Record. After publishing a book of poetry, Taylor would go on to wander Europe on foot and to write about his experiences for the New York Tribune, and would wander the globe as a journalist, poet and lecturer of great fame, but that is a story for another day. This is the story of Enos, whose life's journey was launched by the death of his father.

Enos took well to newspaper work and thoroughly enjoyed the camaraderie of his fellow apprentices. He might have been content to finish out his indenture and stay on at the Record as a career, as meager

Enos Christman is shown in this
daguerreotype made in California on
Oct. 26, 1851.

the income might be, if it were not for one significant distraction. Her name was Ellen Apple.

Ellen A. Martin was born in Philadelphia in 1829. Her mother died when she was just a toddler, and so she was sent to West Chester to be raised by the family of her uncle, Capt. William Apple, as one of their own. She was known to all as Ellen Apple.

Enos Christman and Ellen began courting as teenagers, and by the time Enos had completed several years of his apprenticeship, they pledged themselves to one another. Marriage would have to wait, however, until Enos could manage to make a good enough living to support her – not a likely prospect as a small-town printer working for someone else.

It was near the end of his fourth year at the Record when Gold Fever struck Enos. After the discovery of the precious metal at Sutter's Mill, thousands of men dropped everything and headed for California, inebriated with the desire to strike it rich. Enos saw this not just as an opportunity to flee the drudgery of the print but as a way to make enough money to enable him to return home financially secure enough to marry Ellen.

Of course, getting to California was a problem. There was the matter of his bound position at the Record, and the journey there – by sail around the southern tip of South America – would be costly. Where would he get the money for that?

Much to Enos' surprise, Record owner Henry Evans shared his young charge's enthusiasm, released him from his job and advanced him $400 for the voyage, gambling on the prospect that Enos would make a fortune in the gold fields, much to the benefit of his backer.

And so in late June 1849, Enos Christman left West Chester and Ellen to begin what they both knew would be a long and perilous journey. They both realized that he would be gone for years. They could never know, however that this was also the beginning of a great love story.

Enos Christman booked passage on the clipper ship Europe, but its departure from the Philadelphia port was delayed for several days. While waiting, Enos exchanged letters with Ellen and fellow apprentice Peebles Prizer and learned that his good friend DeWitt Clinton Atkins would be joining him on the voyage.

The couple's prolonged parting proved painful. "I had a daguerreotype likeness taken, which will be sent to you with this," Enos wrote Ellen on June 30, 1849. "Take it, and may it ever be a source of comfort to you. Should I have the good luck ever to return, I hope the mutual pledges given by us may be fulfilled, and believe me that I cannot change. My feelings at parting now, you can better imagine than I can describe."

Ellen was candid in her reaction, writing on July 1: "I return many, many thanks for your likeness. You could not have sent me anything which would have been half so valuable. When I look upon it, it will serve to call up pleasant recollections of the past. But I shall need nothing to remind me of you. The likeness is most excellent but what an unspeakable pleasure it would have been to have taken one more look at the original. I must bear the trial and keep it to myself. I must appear cheerful and indifferent while my anxiety for your future comfort is beyond description…"

The Europe departed the harbor on July 4. It would not reach San Francisco for another 221 days. Enos had anticipated stormy seas, seasickness and even regret of his decisions during a voyage of many months, but he could never have imagined what else he and Atkins would endure before their feet once again touched land.

Enos Christman, his friend Atkins and most of the other 50 passengers aboard the Europe suffered from seasickness through the first two months of the voyage. After passing the equator on Aug. 31, boredom set in, followed by peril. Following are a few snippets from Christman's journal:

Sept. 9 - There is nothing to be seen from one end to the other but a dreary waste of blue sky above the rolling water below… But notwithstanding all that has been said of its charms, its novelty is now over and it hath no charms any longer for me. It is nearly 10 weeks since we left port. Truly a long time to see nothing but sky and water and our own good ship, and yet it will be a long while again before we reach port…

Sept. 30 – Deep, low mutterings usually ensue after meals, and not without cause, as this is an almost intolerable place as far as table luxuries are concerned. Our bread now contains worms half an inch in length, and is a little musty, and out duff is very badly cooked, not better than mere dough heated. Complaint was made to the Captain and he gave us directions to flog the cook next time it came to us in such a manner. I shall go to bed supperless. I have been much below par and in bed the greater part of the day.

Oct. 21 – A tremendous wave struck the vessel Tuesday morning, covering the deck with several feet of water and rolling some of the passengers from side to side, ducking them most thoroughly. The same wave rolled a volume of water down the hatchway, covering the greater part of our cabin with three to six inches, which floated some of the trunks about and wet some of their contents… Friday morning the startling announcement was made that on account of this continual tossing about by the storms and waves, we had unexpectedly lost about 1,400 gallons of water out of a large square iron tank and as a consequence, the passengers would be allowed but one quart per day for all purposes...

Dec. 19 – Yesterday afternoon, Mr. Sterling's little boy met with a slight fall, and in the evening he was seized with a severe fit... About 11 o'clock this forenoon the child died. This afternoon his body was sewed up in a piece of canvas, with three cannon balls at the feet to make it sink, and then placed on a plank with the American flag around it... and his mortal remains were cast into the ocean.

Jan. 12 – While lying in the harbor in Valparaiso (Chile) we were almost devoured by fleas, but we were not troubled long after we left. Since then a new scourge has been sent to trouble us. For a few weeks past some have been unable to sleep on account of something biting and creeping over them. Upon search they found their bunks to be infested with bedbugs of monstrous growth and great numbers...

Feb. 7 – About nine o'clock the joyful cry of "Land, ho!" was heard and by going aloft to the fore-topsail guard, I was able to see the dim outline of several ridges of land. At the first sight of the land of promise, oh how my heart leaped with joy!

But for Enos and his friend, their greater hardship was only just beginning.

Enos Christman found San Francisco an exciting place, although outrageously expensive. "Gambling here is an occupation, day and night, Sunday or any other time," he wrote in his journal on Feb. 22, 1850. "The grey-headed father and the beardless boy are seen side by side vying with each other who can win or lose the fastest, and even

This engraving of the Europe, on which Enos Christman and friend Clint Atkins spent 221 days on their journey from Philadelphia to San Francisco, is taken from a bill of lading in Christman's papers.

beautiful women engage in these games with the same earnestness of the sterner sex, betting their last ounce. I have even heard of preachers delivering a good sermon and going directly from the pulpit to the gaming table… Money here goes like dirt. Everything costs a dollar or dollars. What is considered a fortune at home is here mere pocket money, Today I purchased a single potato for 45 cents."

Prospecting for gold was not all that it was cracked up to be, Enos discovered. He and Atkins left San Francisco by steamer up the Sacramento River on March 11 and began an overland trek to the foothills of the Sierra Nevada range a week later. "Our long voyage at sea unfitted us for such a tramp and hence we have been almost worn out, but a day or two's rest, we hope, will restore our usual vigor." Enos wrote on March 19. "For the past few days Atkins was apparently improving rapidly, but today he took a relapse and I fear he may have a hard sickness…"

Rest never came. For weeks they traveled slowly through rain and across swollen streams, through land tracked by grizzlies, wolves and hostile Indians and bandits, to the high ground of the gold fields. When they finally reached Mariposa, pickings were slim.

Panning for gold proved to be backbreaking labor, a day's work often yielding not enough gold dust to buy even a loaf of bread. Through the spring, Atkins remained too ill to work. They sold off much of their belongings for food and soon were down to almost nothing.

May 9, 1850 – "While going up to camp to get my dinner, I saw the express wagon pass down towards the city. I expected letters by it and immediately after dinner I put all the money I had, seven dollars, in my pocket and went down to the express office and enquired for the letters. Four were handed me at two dollars each, making eight dollars. I paid the seven I had and asked them to trust me for the other until evening, knowing that I had five dollars due me for a day's work last week…"

Enos and Atkins followed other prospectors in a search for better

diggings, or some other way to make money. Their trek took them near
Stockton on June 1. It was there, after 11 months of hardship, poverty,
illness bad luck and grueling work that the sun finally began to shine
on Enos Christman.

Around Stockton, there was a lot more money in harvesting hay
than in panning for gold. Enos Christman hit the fields, but "Atkins is
still too sick to work," he wrote in his journal in June 1, 1850. "But rich
or poor as long as he is sick I shall stick by him and it shall never be
said of me that I deserted a friend when health and fortune failed."

A few days later, Enos found work "sticking type" at the Stockton
Times. The money was good – about $50 a week. The Times also
began printing the first newspaper to serve the gold fields – the
Sonora Herald - on July 4, and Enos was sent there to sell the papers.
Eventually, the old Ramage press, which had printed the Californian,
the first newspaper in that state, was sent up to Sonora, where Enos
operated it along with editor Lewis Gunn. The two would eventually
become partners and owners of the Herald.

There was no shortage of news or other jobs to print. The business
of elections was brisk, particularly with California becoming a state.
And then there were the Indian raids, the rampages of Mexican
bandits, frequent murders and the swift justice of vigilance committees
and lynch mobs when horse thieves were caught.

The letters, which usually took two months to be delivered,
continued to flow between Enos and Ellen Apple, she always pleading
for his return, he always maintaining that he would stay long enough to
return well enough off to repay his former employer's investment.

Ellen to Enos, July 14, 1850 - "…Dear Enos, you have made every

THE TWO MEN STANDING IN THE DOORWAY
OF THIS PHOTO OF THE SONORA HERALD ARE
UNIDENTIFIED BUT COULD WELL BE LEWIS
GUNN AND ENOS CHRISTMAN.

effort to obtain gold. You have failed in the effort. Be not disheartened. Riches taketh wings and flies away but happiness no one can take away from us. I repeat what I have said in all my letters, that it is not every man's luck to make a fortune. If your health has improved and you have a safe return to your dearest friends, to have made the effort will perhaps be a lasting benefit and repay you for all your trouble. I have told you that a living can be made in Chester County and gold will not buy health and happiness..."

Enos to Ellen, Oct. 6, 1850 – "... Advise me to stay and try my luck another season, and in a year from now I promise to be with you. Or beneath the waves of the ocean, or my bones bleaching on the plains, if Providence should so will it..."

Enos to Ellen, Oct. 26, 1851 – "This morning I concluded to have my likeness taken, and I forward it with this to you. I am only sorry that it is not the original that is to go and the likeness to remain..."

Ellen to Enos, Dec. 8, 1851 – "How shall I express the unexpected joy I felt when I received your kind letter accompanied with your daguerreotype. You could have sent nothing except yourself, that would have been half so acceptable. Although it was a great pleasure to receive it, it made me feel rather sad to see how much thinner you are. But, oh, that awful California is enough to wear flesh and bones away..."

Enos Christman was now living comfortably in the adobe building that housed the Sonora Herald, along with Lewis Gunn and his family, who had made the long sea journey to join him. He and Gunn were now partners and owners of the newspaper, and real success seemed not so many years distant. But Ellen's siren call was getting to him. As summer approached in 1852, Enos began making plans to go home.

On June 26, nearly three years to the day from when he left West Chester, Enos left San Francisco on a clipper bound for Panama, leaving behind his friend Atkins to seek his fortune in gold. Enos planned to take the short cut, traveling by horseback across the Isthmus, despite the danger that involved.

After crossing to the east coast of Panama, Enos boarded a steamer bound for New Orleans and New York. The trip would be comparatively quick, but the human cost high. "Tuesday, July 20 - A terrible day on board," he wrote in his journal. "There have been seven or eight deaths and burials, and a large addition to the sick-list." The next day, he wrote: "There are two new cases of sickness, and two deaths today... My clean shirts were stolen."

Cholera claimed 17 lives on the El Dorado before it docked on July 22 in New York Harbor. As Providence would have it, Enos Christman was not one of them.

After Enos returned home to West Chester, he repaid his former employer's advance, with interest, and he and Ellen were married on Oct. 20, 1852. They departed immediately for Washington, Pa., where Enos would take up an offer from a former fellow apprentice, George Stouch, to be his partner in a new newspaper, The Commonwealth, espousing the cause of the Whig party.

Not long after their arrival there, Enos received a grievous letter from John L. Haines in Sonora, Calif. "I am writing for the purpose of conveying to you the melancholy news of the death of D.W. Clinton Atkins, your fellow traveler through many trying times during your sojourn in this far-off land," the letter stated. "...on Christmas morning I thought I would go to see him and spend the day. It is impossible to describe my surprise when arriving at his cabin, blocked up with snow, I found him there alone, covered with smallpox and totally blind. He was sitting over his stove with a blanket around him and scarcely any fire. As soon as he became aware of my presence, he burst out crying and said, 'I am glad you have come for I thought I was to die here by myself and my cabin be my grave.'"

Atkins died on Jan. 4, 1853. Enos could not help recalling him when he and Ellen, then about 6 months pregnant, returned to the Philadelphia area for a visit and went down to the port to see the clipper Europe, on which the two young men had begun their adventure.

"What trying times those were for Atkins and myself," Enos wrote in his journal on May 9, 1853. "It is a true saying that health is the greatest of blessings. How easy it was for Clint to walk into trouble. He saw more hardships in three years than in his whole life before, and he breathed his last in a lonely cabin in that far-off land.

"But the thought of the dear burthen on my arm broke into my musings and reminded me that all was well with me. Indeed, my hopes have been gratified and I have realized a fortune."

For Enos and Ellen, their life together had just begun, and all did indeed seem well. It would not stay that way for very long, however.

It was cholera that had decimated the passengers on the steamer that brought Enos Christman back from the gold fields. And it was cholera that would cast its shadow on the door of the Christman home on West Chestnut Street in Washington two years later.

Ellen had given birth to her first child, Mary Elizabeth, on Aug. 15, 1853. Just 13 months later, the dreaded disease took the baby's life. She was buried in Washington Cemetery when there were but few graves. As years went by, other members of the family would join her in that plot. There are no stones or markers there today. She lies beneath a grassy patch in the shade of a giant fir, overlooking the south and east of the city.

Not quite nine months later, the Christmans' second daughter, Sarah, was born in the house where they were then living on West Beau Street.

Enos and George Stouch managed to do well with the Commonwealth, despite the split and turmoil in the Whig party since the election of 1852. Their partnership came to an end, however, when Stouch died of tuberculosis on Dec. 28, 1855.

"He was a gentleman of fine social qualities – of generous impulses and a fine sense of honor," the obituary in The Reporter stated. "He has left a partner and one child with a large train of devoted friends to deplore his early call from the walks of life."

George Stouch was 28 years old.

Enos needed an editor and partner and found a capable one in William Moore, a 1848 graduate of Washington College. But following the 1856 election, the Whigs, once championed by Henry Clay and Abraham Lincoln, were reduced to an ineffective third party and dissolved, leaving the Commonwealth without cause or readership. By 1858, about the time the Christmans' son William was born, the Commonwealth merged with The Reporter, and Christman and Moore shared ownership of the latter with Robert Strean.

Later in 1858, the Christmans left Washington and returned to West Chester, where Enos went to work as foreman for his old employer, Henry Evans, at The Village Record. Curiously, Enos did not sell his interest in The Reporter, a decision that would have a significant impact on Washington's future.

Ellen gave birth to another daughter, Elizabeth, in 1859, and she was pregnant with Ella in April 1861 when the darkest days in America began, when Enos would be pulled away from her again, not to return for years.

In May 1861, Enos Christman helped organize Company K of the Fourth Regiment, Pennsylvania Reserve Volunteer Corps, and was elected second lieutenant. He would not come marching home for two years.

In that time, Enos fought in the battles in front of Richmond known as Seven Days, the Second Bull Run, South Mountain and Fredericksburg. He also survived the bloodiest day in U.S. military history – Antietam. He would learn much later that on that day he fought in the same vicinity as his two brothers, William and Jefferson, none of whom was injured. He was promoted to captain, and then to major, and then President Lincoln sent him home to West Chester in May 1863 to serve as provost marshal of the Seventh District until the end of the war.

It seemed that West Chester had a gravitational pull that Enos could not escape, although he kept trying. At war's end, Enos and Ellen took their six children to Somerset County, Md., to try their hand at farming. It was a hard life, made more difficult by drought.

William, Enos' oldest son, recalled in an article in The Reporter in 1908 that he attended school only occasionally, when he was not needed for work on the farm. He spent many an hour riding a horse, while his father followed with the plow, working corn, and hauling and chopping cordwood.

Four years later, the Christmans gave up and surrendered to the pull of home, where Enos once again took up the printing trade at the West Chester Republican. The children kept coming and by 1872 numbered eight. It seemed that they were destined to live out their lives in West Chester, until in November a letter arrived from Enos' old partner in Washington, Pa., William Moore. It was a letter that would have a profound effect on the Christman family and would alter the course of local history.

William Moore was elected to Congress on the Republican ticket in the fall of 1872. His partner James Kelley would be unable to take over The Reporter in his absence, and so Moore wrote to Enos Christman, who still owned an interest in the paper, and pleaded with his to return to Washington.

The Christmans, after a 15-year hiatus, returned to Washington, and Enos took over as editor and manager on April 2, 1873. His son William, then 15, who had been such a help to his father on the farm, and then delivering newspapers in West Chester, attended school for only three weeks before quitting and going to work for his father. It would be a career that lasted 30 years to the day.

It was Enos' need to find a suitable home in Washington for his large family and his inability to afford one that led to his founding the first building and loan association here. His house at 21 West Prospect Avenue, which still stands, was in 1874 the first to be built by the Washington Building & Loan Association. Before that pioneer institution passed out of existence, it had made possible the building of many homes and businesses in Washington and was an inspiration to the lending institutions that would follow.

Clark Bartlett, who worked as an editor for Christman, wrote in 1925 of his former employer: "The Major was by nature thrifty and conservative, yet courageously progressive when occasion demanded."

That courage would be put to the test when Christman launched Washington's first daily newspaper in 1876. Many of his competitors and business associates thought that venture was foolish and destined to fail.

And they were nearly right.

PUBLISHER WILLIAM MOORE, ELECTED
TO CONGRESS IN 1872, ASKED ENOS
CHRISTMAN TO RETURN TO WASHINGTON
TO RUN THE REPORTER.

THE STREAN BUILDING, WHICH STILL STANDS
ON SOUTH MAIN STREET, HOUSED THE
REPORTER WHEN CHRISTMAN RETURNED TO
WASHINGTON IN 1873.

The Chinese and Koreans were using moveable type as early as 1200, but Gutenberg introduced it to Europe in 1436. In 1876, type was still being set the same way: by hand, one letter at a time. That's what made printing a daily newspaper such a daunting endeavor.

It was one thing to print a four-page weekly newspaper, and quite another to do it six days a week. A printer was able to set only about 2 columns of type in a day, so producing four 6-column pages required two people working six days a week. A daily paper would require six times the workforce, but Washington was still a small town at the time, and there was no way to find six times as many advertisers or to convince advertisers to spend six times as much.

Enos Christman's business model was risky. Instead of printing his daily on the big sheets of paper to which his readers were accustomed, he would print a daily newspaper half the size, with half the type. It quickly gained the derisive nickname, "The Dinky." This paper was distributed only in the city. A twice-weekly, regular-size newspaper, using the already-set type from the daily and also called The Reporter, was distributed to outlying areas. In doing so, the paper would gain a huge advantage in timeliness over his weekly rivals.

Launching the daily was an experiment, conducted in total secrecy. The appearance of carriers on the street on Friday, Aug. 4, 1876, was a complete surprise to the public. The paper announced: "We propose delivering it free of charge at every house, office, store and shop in town for a week or 10 days for the purpose of giving the people an opportunity of seeing what the publication will be. If it is continued longer it will be one cent per copy or six cents per week. No one will be forced to take it."

Almost 1,000 copies were distributed each day during the trial. At least 500 paid subscribers were needed to continue the daily, and they got them, though just barely. When Aug. 4, 1877, rolled around, Christman and Moore had accumulated between 800 and 1,000 subscribers and announced that the experiment had proved successful and the daily newspaper would continue.

Two months later, his health failing, William Moore announced the sale of his interest in The Reporter, and on Dec. 30, 1877, he died. Five years later, Enos gained complete ownership of the business and began looking for ways to grow not just the newspaper, but the community.

That growth would be enormous, and it would all start with a few bubbles escaping from the bed of Chartiers Creek.

Early settlers in this area dug wells to reach brine water, which provided them salt, a valuable commodity. Natural gas and oil were occasionally found when digging these wells, but it was not until 1882, when the Niagara Drilling Co. struck gas at 2,300 feet near Hickory that the extent of the reserves could be guessed.

That well became known as the Mighty McGugin. The roar of the gas escaping and burning could be heard as far away as Washington, and it would not be successfully capped and put to use for four years.

Inspired by this discovery, Enos Christman and four other Washington businessmen decided to drill a well closer to the city in hopes of using that gas to heat and light their businesses and homes. Some of the men remembered as boys swimming in the Old Kettle Hole in Chartiers Creek. They would often amuse themselves by lighting the gas the bubbled up from the creek bottom. They formed the Peoples Light & Heat Co. and chose a site near there on the Hess farm, west of Jefferson Avenue behind what is now Ann's Feeds, and began drilling in March 1884. They struck a pocket that would prove

ENOS CHRISTMAN IN HIS LATER YEARS, AND
SON WILLIAM.

ENOS AND ELLEN CHRISTMAN ARE
BURIED UNDER THIS MONUMENT IN
WASHINGTON CEMETERY.

to be as productive as the McGugin.

Laying pipe moved with incredible speed. By July 1, the first connections were made to businesses in the borough of Washington. By the end of the month, 46 homes, including that of the Christman family, had gas service.

It was the availability of natural gas that attracted industry to Washington, with the first of several large glass factories started here in 1888. The gas strike inspired other drilling and the discovery of large reserves of oil. At one point, 18,575 barrels a day were being pumped from the Washington field.

Washington became a boomtown. Many became millionaires and the population exploded. The Peoples gas company grew and became Manufacturers Light & Heat, which eventually became the Columbia Gas System. And Enos Christman, pretty much forgotten these past 100 years, had much to do with that.

The Christman Publishing Co. was formed in 1891, with Enos as president and son William as manager. It was under William's direction that The Reporter five years later purchased a Cox Duplex press able to print 4,000 copies and hour. In 1897, two Mergenthaler Linotype machines were put into operation. Each machine cost $8,000 and could set type at more than four times the speed of a human printer. Later that year, Enos turned over ownership of company to his children, William, Elizabeth and Harry.

On May 6, 1899, after a lingering illness, Ellen died. She had born Enos nine children, eight of whom survived. She had been the light of Enos' life for 50 years. Her death was the end of a great love story, but not the end of Enos' love. He would marry and bury another woman,

Catherine Stofer, and marry a third time, to Emma Winebrenner, before Enos himself died at age 83 on Jan. 12, 1912.

William Christman would sell The Reporter to the Observer Publishing Co. in 1903 and quit the business 30 years to the day after he quit school to work for his father at the newspaper. But Christmans would continue to work at The Reporter and the Observer-Reporter for generations to come. The last of the family to work at the paper was photographer Ron Christman, who died in a helicopter crash in 1973 while taking aerial photos for the paper's Progress Edition.

Enos Christman, the old prospector, spent the last days of his life in the home he built on the aptly named Prospect Avenue. The old love story came to light many years after his death when his letters and journal were examined. In the introduction to "One Man's Gold: The Letters and Journal of a Forty Niner," niece Florence Morrow Christman in 1930 wrote:

"The tin box had no air of mystery although it had stood for three-quarters of a century in a dark closet under the stairs of an old Pennsylvania house. It was just a tin box – square-topped and high, double-padlocked and rusted. Everyone knew that all it contained were old letters and papers. It had been designed by one who had gone adventuring, to guard the records of his journeyings. But when his voice had become a memory, the old box was drawn from its corner, and again the dreams and the experiences of Enos Christman lived."

So much has happened in the century since Enos Christman died, yet so much of what he made remains: the house on West Prospect Avenue, the gas company, and most of all, the newspaper. Many newspapers have come and gone from Washington; only one remains. It has published continuously since 1808 – daily since 1876 – and never missed a publication date.

It's likely that this newspaper would not exist today if it were not for Enos and for Ellen, who convinced him of the broader definition of gold.

CHAPTER FIVE

Enter, With Torches

The Scene: Mrs. LaRosa's first-grade classroom at Public School No. 30, Yorkers, N.Y. It is January 1955. Thirty-five noisy children become quiet when their teacher claps her hands.

Mrs. LaRosa: All right, settle down boys and girls. I need two more volunteers for our zoo. Who would like to dress up like an animal tomorrow and have your classmates guess what animal you are?

These earliest memories are different in that I don't recall things as I saw them. Instead, I see myself from a distance. I am this hovering spirit from the future that floats into the classroom and contemplates a boy-child in Buster Brown oxfords and a too-tight flannel shirt, his hair punctuated by a cowlick.

The boy is a new student, his family having just moved to the area from Connecticut. He hasn't made friends yet with anyone in his class. When Mrs. LaRosa asks for volunteers, his arm flies up and she chooses him. She chooses one of the girls, too, and she takes them out into the hall and whispers to them, "You can be a monkey, Susan, and you can be a seal."

Next day, the boy arrives at school with a beach ball and a costume his mother put together the night before from gray flannel. Mrs. LaRosa says, "You and Susan, quickly, go into the cloakroom and change into your costumes." Among all the coats and boots, Susan strips, and the boy stands petrified. Presently, Mrs. LaRosa enters. "What are you doing just standing there? Quickly, take off your pants and shirt and get into your costume!"

The boy thinks: Take off my pants, in front of a girl? And let her see me in my underwear? Reluctantly, he turns his back to Susan, nuzzles as far into the coats as he can and slips out of his trousers and into the flannel.

The boy scoots out of the cloakroom on his hands and knees, pushing the beach ball with his nose. When he reaches the front of the class, he climbs onto a chair and flaps his flippers and barks. "He's a seal!" they all scream.

The boy keeps barking until Mrs. LaRosa tells him to stop it and go get dressed. He is euphoric. Now they will look at him and laugh and remember him and be his friends. It was all worth it, he thinks, even being seen in his underwear by a girl.

The scene: The living room of an apartment, three years later. The furniture is Danish Modern with a blond finish. In one corner is a bar-on-wheels with seltzer bottles, and along one wall a "hi-fi." On the sofa sit a couple in their 30s, reading.

The boy enters the room, wearing his mother's sunglasses, his father's smoking jacket and a towel wrapped around his neck in the fashion of an ascot. In his hands are a Meerschaum pipe and a sheaf of papers – the script for an elementary school play. He struts about the room, huffing and a-hemming until his parents take notice. They stare in silent bemusement.

"If anyone should call, my agent or my producer for instance," the boy says in an attempt at a haughty British accent, "please inform them that I am too busy for them now. I'm studying my lines. We have a rehearsal, tomorrow, after all."

Miss Fletcher's fourth-grade class is staging the play, "A Rhyme for Orange." The boy has one of the larger speaking roles, and he is thrilled by the idea of performing on the stage in front of the whole school. The play, probably written by Miss Fletcher herself, climaxes with a song by the entire class, and then the lines, delivered by the boy with a flourish, that reveal the word that rhymes with orange.

When the boy shouts out these closing lines in rehearsal, his classmates scrunch their faces and look at each other as if they'd just smelled something bad.

"Grange?"

"That doesn't rhyme with orange!"

"What's a grange?" they all ask.

Miss Fletcher tries to explain that a grange is a farmhouse, and if you don't pronounce it as if it rhymes with "strange," then it does rhyme with orange. She seems a little panicked by the reaction of her pupils.

She instructs the class to settle down and start again, from the song. The boy hears his classmates giggling: "That's just plain stupid!" one of them blurts out. "This is the dumbest play I ever heard of," another says.

The boy feels deep sympathy for his teacher and playwright, and anger at his fellow cast members for their derisive comments.

"Critics!" he mutters.

My family moved in 1958 from the apartment to a house a couple of miles away. I changed schools from the fairly new, single-floor P.S. 30 to the one in our new neighborhood, P.S. 8 – an ugly monster of a building constructed in 1896, where the wooden desks were bolted to the floors and had ink wells, and where the stairwells smelled of sour milk and Murphy's Oil Soap.

Each year, the eighth graders put on a show to which the entire school was invited. When I was in sixth grade, it was announced that their performance would be a musical variety show. I dreaded becoming an eighth-grader and being asked to sing a song on stage in front of all of my friends, who would tease me for being in a dopey musical and call me a fairy. But I changed my mind about that when I watched as Brian Carney, whose father played Ed Norton on Jackie Gleason's show, "The Honeymooners," strut across the stage singing, "Pennies from Heaven." After that, I don't think there was a girl in school who was not in love with Brian Carney.

I liked girls, a lot. They didn't notice me. All the girls in my class were about a foot taller than I was, at age 11. At eye level, I saw their collar bones, and they saw, well, Brian Carney in the distance. I figured if I could learn to sing, the girls would love me, too, even though my father wasn't a TV star. And I didn't hear any boys calling Brian Carney a fairy.

So, I started paying attention in music class and was the most eager participant when we sang as a choir. My voice had yet to change; I was in the alto section.

"You there, tone it down a bit," the music teacher said, pointing to me.

"A little quieter," she ordered me later.

When we resumed the song, I did nothing but move my lips.

"That's much better," she said to me with a little smile.

It became clear to me that my voice would never allow me to bask in the adulation of appreciative audiences, and have girls swoon over me.

I'd have to find an easier way.

Even in 1966, "Arsenic and Old Lace" was an old warhorse of a play, a favorite of schools and community theater groups. Written by Joseph Kesselring in 1939, and made by Frank Capra into a popular film five years later staring Cary Grant, it is a humorous and somewhat creepy tale of two sweet old ladies who take pathetic, lonely old men into their Victorian home, poison them with arsenic-laced elderberry wine and employ their deranged nephew to bury the "yellow fever victims" in the cellar.

The Darrow School production was a bit different because it was performed by an all-male cast. Almost all of our theater productions were all male, because Darrow was a boys' school, and the only women around were a handful of faculty wives. Occasionally, one of those women would consent to join the cast, but for the most part we were limited to single-sex plays like "Stalag 17."

This was my first real play. By that, I mean a production where you have costumes, make-up, sets, lighting and a director. There was a method to rehearsing, I learned. It wasn't anything like grade school or those rainy-summer-afternoon dramas we produced as kids, ala the Little Rascals.

You started out sitting in a circle and reading the play, with each actor reading his own lines. Then the play is "blocked" – which can take several nights of rehearsal. That's when the director decides where the actors enter and exist the stage, where they move on the stage, and where the furniture and props will be located, and all these spots are marked with masking tape on the stage floor. Then rehearsals start, with actors reading from their scripts; then the scripts are cast away; then the dress rehearsals; and finally the first performance.

I played one of the gentlemen callers – the victims – in "Arsenic

Characters Abby and Martha Brewster
prepare elderberry wine in the Darrow
production of "Arsenic and Old Lace."

and Old Lace." It was a small role, but I was so proud to be part of a play that was hilarious and a hit with the student body.

It was casting that made the production such a success; in particular, the selection of the two boys who played the little old ladies. These were boys who were sometimes teased because of their effeminate demeanor. They actually behaved like little old ladies in real life. I think the other students were impressed by the sportsmanship of these two boys, who poured their own personalities and mannerisms into their roles and risked humiliation to do so. The harshest words I ever heard about their performance were, "They were perfect for their parts."

The genius behind the casting was our director, a man whose own personality and mannerisms might have subjected him to ridicule as well, if he were not such an admired and inspiring teacher.

Night after night, we practiced our play to an audience of one. Sometimes, when the spotlight was in our eyes we could not see him there, our director, but we felt his presence, his attention, and we could smell the smoke from his Chesterfields, their butts lying crushed beside his shoes.

The Darrow School stage jutted out into a semicircle of concrete levels. There were no seats because when the building in which the theater was housed was built a few years earlier, the money ran out before seats could be purchased. During performances, some folding chairs were brought in for women, the elderly and the important, and everyone else made cushions of their coats and sat on the cold concrete.

So our director, Ronald Emery, sat on the edge of one of these levels, leaning forward with elbows on knees, in a blue cloud of cigarette smoke, barking out encouragement and admonishment.

He was a pudgy, balding man in his early 30s who, because of some affliction, dragged his right foot as he walked. He seemed to waddle as he rushed down from his perch in the auditorium, vaulted onto the stage, pushed aside an actor and performed the bit as he wanted it done. To watch him doing one of the Brewster sisters in "Arsenic Old Lace," you'd almost believe he was a grandmother in an earlier life. He seemed prissy, effete and middle-aged to us, although we were not that much younger than he.

But Mr. Emery was much more to us than a director. Like almost all the faculty at Darrow, he lived on campus in one of the old Shaker buildings we used as dormitories, and the strains of Wagner, Rachmaninov and Mahler could usually be heard emanating from behind his apartment door late into the night.

He taught sophomore English and did so with a passion few teachers can rival. For some of us, our love of drama and poetry and the English language sprouted in his classroom. Most of us remember a teacher whose influence changed the course of our life. I had several favorite teachers, but none had more effect on me. He made me a reader and a writer, and so what you are reading at this very moment would not exist if it were not for Ronald Emery.

After the fall production of "Arsenic and Old Lace," a few of us came down with theater fever. We simply couldn't wait until the next official school production in the spring, so we staged our own plays.

You need to understand that we had nothing better to do with our free time than put on plays. Because Darrow was an all-boys school, we had no distraction from the opposite sex, and being situated on the side of a mountain in the Berkshires, surrounded by forest and farm

RONALD EMERY. ENGLISH TEACHER AND
DRAMATIC DIRECTOR, TAUGHT US TO SOAR.

TONY CLARK, LEFT, WAS LENNY AND PARKER
BURROUGHS PLAYED GEORGE IN THE DARROW
PRODUCTION OF "OF MICE AND MEN."

fields, miles from any town, we were cut off from the world, with no newspapers or radio or television to entertain us. When we weren't required to be in classrooms, study halls, on the playing fields or in our beds with lights out at 10 o'clock, we needed to find things to keep our minds and bodies busy or risk going mad from cabin fever, homesickness and boredom.

We wrote and staged our own play, "Circus of Sour," a series of ridiculous sketches that we imagined rivaled the best in the latest trend in drama – the theater of the absurd. We had, um, expansive imaginations.

Ronald Emery had introduced us to John Steinbeck in sophomore English class, and so we seized upon the stage version of his novel, "Of Mice and Men," for another all-student production that winter. The play was convenient in that it had just one female role, and we managed to talk the wife of one of the younger masters into taking it.

Because I had one of the main roles, I invited my parents to opening night. Fortunately, after their three-hour drive from home, they were able to sit on chairs in the auditorium rather than on bare concrete slabs. After the curtain came down and I had cleaned off my greasepaint, I bounded up to the back of the auditorium, anxious to find my parents and ask them what they had thought of my performance. I found my mother rubbing the small of her back with both hands.

"Yeah, it was good," she said. "But three hours! Jeez, Louise! Three hours!"

Oh, I thought. Oh, my, she's right. Our student director had not cut a single line from the script. No wonder we were never able to rehearse the play in its entirety before lights-out.

We thought we had produced a masterpiece, all on our own. Instead, it was a monster. We hadn't even considered our audience and the atmosphere in which they would experience our play.

They say you learn from your mistakes. If so, we learned an awful lot at Darrow.

We weren't enthused when Ronald Emery announced that the spring production would be "Antigone." This was a Greek tragedy written by Sophocles 2,500 years ago, and here we were, in the middle of the 20th century, with the world ready to be pulverized by nuclear weapons, just a few months short of the "Summer of Love," and we're doing Sophocles?

Actually, Mr. Emery had chosen a newer version of the play, written by Jean Anouilh, in which the characters dressed and spoke in contemporary fashion, rather than shouting their lines from behind giant masks, as Greek drama was originally presented. But not having had my fill of the theater yet, I showed up for the tryouts.

We were asked to read several of the parts and were puzzled because at least three of the roles were female. "Are we going to have to wear wigs and pretend to be girls in this play, too?" someone asked. Then Mr. Emery said something that shocked us silent. He told us that the female roles would be played by girls from Miss Hall's School.

Only those who have been sequestered far away from the opposite sex for long periods can imagine the excitement and anticipation that coursed through our veins at that moment. Suddenly, our interest in "Antigone" was intense and our reading of the script inspired. We secretly congratulated ourselves for having the foresight to show up for try-outs. Even if we didn't get parts in the play, we would be allowed to be stage hands or build the sets or do the lighting and be around real live girls in practices, night after night. Ah, the poor slobs who turned

HEADMASTER JOHN JOLINE AND MARY HALL,
MOTHER OF MY ROOMMATE, DEAN, REACT TO
STAGE ANTICS AT DARROW IN 1967.

their noses up at the spring production!

I landed one of the major roles, that of the Chorus, the narrator of the tragedy, but it really didn't matter to me what part I got. There would be girls, and that's what mattered most.

Or so I thought.

Oh, to be 18 years old and to fall in love – with just about any girl who showed up on campus! Early one April evening in 1967, four of them appeared at Darrow, arriving in a car driven by a matronly chaperone. They parked and then walked the gantlet between Wickersham and Brethrens' Workshop, boys three-deep at their dormitory windows, gawking at the visitors, the only sounds being the whispering of the breeze in the pines and the crunch of gravel beneath their delicate shoes.

We were waiting for the girls from Miss Hall's School in the Dairy Barn, which housed our theater. It was a new building and not a barn at all, but it was built on the site of the old dining hall-theater-gym, which before the fire that destroyed it was indeed a dairy barn, used by the Shakers who populated these buildings through all of the 19th century.

We tried our best to look nonchalant, even bored. We kept our eyes on the director and examined the newcomers only in our peripheral vision. But there was no escaping the sexual energy that charged the atmosphere of our dimly lighted stage.

I loved them all. For four weeks of practice and rehearsals, I reveled in the invisible cloud of girl smell they brought to us. But most of all, there was Hylkia deGreve, who played Ismene. At night I would lie awake past midnight, smiling in the dark, imagining a life together with her.

PARKER BURROUGHS NARRATED "ANTIGONE"
AS THE CHORUS IN THE 1967
DARROW PRODUCTION.

Hylkia de Greve, a student at Miss
Hall's School, played Ismene in
"Antigone."

But this obsession was not mutual. Hylkia was friendly and polite to me, but that's all. Our only backstage intimacy was the sharing of a forbidden cigarette in the dressing room. Still, the sweet melancholy I experienced from this unrequited love was intoxicating. It flowed into the lines I spoke on stage. These emotions gave shape and substance to the words, and the pauses between the words, and I began to understand what acting was all about.

Sadness enveloped most of the cast after our last performance. Graduation was just a few weeks away, and our furious year of theatrics was over. But I was ready to move on. The blinding white heat of the spotlight was something I wasn't ready to give up. I felt ready to begin.

Although I felt ready to take on the collegiate stage, Washington & Jefferson College was not so enthusiastic to take on me. I did not adapt well to the freedom from restrictions that college offered, and my first-semester grades were abominable. In fact, I was placed on academic probation and prohibited from participating in extra-curricular activities, including theater groups.

I joined the Buskin Club in my sophomore year, but as a newcomer, my participation was limited to the stage crew and bit parts with few or no lines. The theater then, in the late 1960s, was in McIlvaine Hall. The stage was small and the wings cramped. The floor of the auditorium was flat, so that all but the audience in the first few rows had trouble seeing what was happening on stage through all the heads in front of them. The dressing and make-up rooms were down a steep flight of stairs and under the stage.

Although the stage itself was inferior to Darrow's, W&J's dramatic efforts were ambitious and its talent deep. What was more exciting was that the college performances were well attended by townspeople, and reviews of plays were actually published in the local newspaper. So, delusions of fame and fortune raced through my head when I finally landed a speaking role, that of the homosexual English painter Nicholas Black in "The Devil's Advocate," a screen adaptation of Morris West's novel.

The shortcomings of our stage were made clear in a review by Lorry Merrill published in the Observer-Reporter in March 1969:

"Another scene that has been sacrificed because of stage space is the climactic moment of Nicholas Black's suicide. How much more effective to have had him leap from the Contessa's balcony to the crags below – as the script demands – than have him exit offstage into the cramped confinement of McIlvaine's wings without even a tremulous scream to punctuate his demise." She added that even "death by pallet knife" would have been preferable.

Further on, she wrote:

"Up to now, Mr. Burroughs has gone unnoticed in lesser roles which evidenced only an adequate capability. Now having had a chance to explore the subtleties of a role requiring cynical overtones and erotic undertones, he clearly demonstrates that he is a more than adequate actor..."

"More than adequate"! I was in heaven. Why, "more than adequate" was almost "good," wasn't it?

Our director, Robert Brindley, was miffed at Merrill's criticism of my stage suicide, so instead of having me stroll offstage during the second performance, he had me leap from the wall of the Contessa's villa. This would have played much better with the audience if I hadn't landed with a loud thud on the other side of the papier-mache wall, eliciting no gasps from the audience, but titters, if not outright laughter.

For the last performance, I went back to strolling offstage to my death. It was less dramatic, but at least we avoided the guffaws.

Although the student body of Washington & Jefferson College was five times larger than that of Darrow School, the two institutions had one thing in common: no women. Both schools would eventually go co-ed, W&J in 1970, but for my first three years of college, theatrical productions had to do without female students.

Just as at Darrow, women from other schools were sometimes recruited, and faculty wives helped out. Kathleen Mitchell, whose husband, R. Lloyd Mitchell taught philosophy, was a fixture in McIlvaine, both on stage as an actress and below the boards handling make-up and costumes. In fact, in "The Devil's Advocate," she played the Contessa, from whose wall I leaped to my death on the stage floor three feet below. And sometimes, for the fun of it, men were cast in female roles, as was the case for "Dirty Work at the Crossroads; or Tempted, Tried and True," which was billed as a gay-nineties melodrama. I had hoped to be able to play the part of the nefarious Munro Murgatroyd, a sort-of Snidely Whiplash character, who might tie his victim, Little Nell, to the railroad tracks if it suited his purposes. Instead, I was assigned the role of Fleurette, the French maid.

I can't recall if I did well in the role, but I can say that I demonstrated profound courage in playing it. Why? Well, picture it:

You're a 20-year-old guy, ready to display you're masculinity whenever it might be questioned. And you're asked to put your short, thick, muscular legs into a pair of fish-net stockings, squeeze into a tiny mini-skirted costume, step into spike heels, put on a wig, rouge and bright red lipstick, stuff your brassiere with rollup-up socks, and then go out on stage in front of an audience of mostly male college students, wait until their howling laughter, cat calls and whistles subside, and then utter lines like, "Ooh, la-la, Masewer, you are so strong, so beeg, so'ansome!"

Courage. Not just for the performance, but to endure the smart-ass remarks that followed it for weeks: "Hey, Fleurette! Where's your feather duster?" and "When ya gonna clean my room, Sweetie?" and "Oh, I didn't recognize you without breasts!"

Eventually, people forgot about "Dirty Work" and my part in it, and it was time for another production – one that would make everything up to that point in my theater experience seem like child's play.

Bemused, annoyed, our director, Peter Skutches, asked me, "What do you think you're doing?"

I had just entered, stage left, with my right arm raised above my head. "Well, it says here in the stage directions that we're supposed to 'enter, with torches'," I answered.

The director scowled at me, his eyelids lowered. Then he put me in my place (the moron closet) for suggesting that we actually carry fire onto the McIlvaine stage and risk roasting 500 innocent theater-goers in a blazing inferno.

So, Shakespeare could be messed with, I learned. We could adapt our production of "Othello" as we saw fit. Drop whole scenes, if we wanted. Have women play the female roles. Cut the long speeches. Lengthen the sword fights. Enter without torches.

From our first night of practice, I knew that doing Shakespeare would be many times more difficult than anything I had done on stage, even though my role – Casio – was not one of the leads. And I realized that Peter Skutches would be nothing like any director I had experienced.

As a professor, pencil-thin and girlish, he could play the clown and make his English Lit classroom rock with laughter. He could also

ENLISH PROFESSOR PETER SKUTCHES
DIRECTED THE WASHINGTON & JEFFERSON
COLLEGE PRODUCTION OF "OTHELLO."

silence a room with a cold stare, and many a student regarded him as a brutal intellectual bully. As a cast, we grew accustomed to the battering.

During one practice, we marched up to our masking-tape marks and recited the lines from our dog-eared scripts. Our director sat a dozen rows back, legs crossed, his foot tapping out an angry rhythm on the earth-brown linoleum.

"Stop!" he shouted. "Put those scripts away! Put them down. Just say your lines. If you can't remember them, just paraphrase."

The actors exchanged worried glances. How were we to know the lines of a Shakespearian play after just three or four nights of practice?

"Continue!" our director yelled.

Silence.

"I thought so," he said, rising and approaching the stage. He berated us for spouting our lines like fountains, completely unaware of their meaning. I felt the burgundy rush of blood to my face, the humiliation, the shame.

When my exit came, I retrieved my script and slipped out into the hallway to start reading the play again, not just for my role but to understand the play as a whole.

Skutches would push us, embarrass us, insult us and keep us on stage well past midnight, night after night, until we got it right. Sometimes, we hated him. But I like to think that some of his brilliance rubbed off on us.

Peter Skutches had me play Casio as foolish, vain and effeminate. Maybe that's why after playing a homosexual painter, a French maid and that prissy part in "Othello," I decided to take a break from acting, for fear of being typecast.

Or maybe doing Shakespeare just exhausted me. All that time in play rehearsals had a serious impact on my grades, and I was again in academic trouble, destined for summer school. Again.

I couldn't give up the stage, though, and instead moved into the wings, working the light board and constructing sets. I had quit the Buskin Club and devoted my time to the Student Experimental Theater, but I spent the remainder of my college days backstage and out of the limelight.

For a while, I mused about a career in the theater. Maybe Broadway was where I should be headed after graduation, although I knew my draft board had something else in mind. That fantasy quickly evaporated, however, when a traveling troupe arrived from New York to stage "Hello, Dolly!" on Trinity High School's stage.

I was in charge of arranging for their transportation from the airport to Washington and getting them to and from their hotel during their stay here, and for their meals and tending to their personal needs. They were demanding people. They were intelligent and entertaining, but they were also obnoxious. How could I attempt a career in the theater if these were the type of people I'd work with? The women were all foul-mouthed and condescending. The men were all egotistical and gay. By comparison, a classroom of unruly children seemed not quite so bad as a workplace for the rest of my life.

After graduation, my bride and I headed for Florida to wait for what seemed then like the inevitable notice from the draft board and an opportunity to spend my time not in the classroom or on the stage but rather in the jungles of Southeast Asia.

I waited, and looked for work – any job that could help support us. Reading the classified ads in the Miami Herald, I found hope for not just work, but the job of dreams.

The advertisement in the Miami Herald was cryptic; it stated only that a motion picture company was conducting casting interviews and listed an address and time. Not only was this a glamorous opportunity, it was a temporary job, so maybe the director might not be so turned off by my draft status, which was 1-A. All my job interviews up to that point ended as soon as the prospective employer asked about the draft and my pathetically low lottery number. I could almost here my application slipping from their fingers and into the waste can.

The address listed in the ad was a second-story office above an empty storefront in a rundown section of Miami. I arrived an hour early, hoping to get a good place in line, but there was no line on the sidewalk, nor on the stairs. Two men and a teenager were standing in the hallway outside an office door, on which hung a sing reading H&R Productions. No one spoke. I did as they did, leaned against a wall the color of soap scum, and stared at my shoes.

I stole glances at the others. One of them was no more than 16 years old, with long, black, greasy hair and a bad case of acne. Another was a college student in neatly pleated chinos and a short-sleeve madras shirt. The third was a man in his 40s with a dark tan, possibly Latino, in a white nylon Dacron dress shirt, gray dress pants and woven leather shoes. His wrists and neck flashed with gold jewelry.

The silence was awkward, and so I asked no one in particular, "Anyone know anything about this company, this movie?" They shrugged and shook their heads apologetically.

By 11 o'clock, the hall was beginning to get warm. We heard the door open and close and footsteps on the stairs. We had long since slid down the wall and had been sitting on the floor, but we all rose and stood at attention for what we figured must be the casting director entering the building. To our disappointment, the new arrivals were a couple – a woman about my age in a dress more suitable for a church social and what appeared to be her husband and protector. "Have the auditions begun yet?" the husband asked.

"There's nobody in there," the teenager croaked.

"But the advertisement said 11 o'clock," the woman protested. We shrugged, and they joined us in silence along the wall.

"Around noon, we heard more footsteps on the stairs and jumped to our feet when we saw two older men, speaking Spanish, appear on the landing. They walked past us as if we were invisible, unlocked the office door, walked in, closed the door and locked it.

We waited. A half hour later, the shorter of the two opened the door slightly, poked his head out and asked, "Are you here to answer the ad?" We all chimed in the affirmative.

"We'll be with you shortly," he said.

A few minutes later, someone threw open the door downstairs and flew up the stairs. "Did he pick his cast yet?" asked a tough-looking thug in his late 20s with a mop of curly blond hair and a fighter's nose. We sighed and gestured toward the door. "Who exactly is he?" the woman asked.

"Who? Jackie? Hernandez? You don't know this guy?" the newcomer laughed. "He's great. He's Cuban. He did "The Old Man and the Sea.""

We were impressed. The grim silence was broken, and we pumped the thug for information. He was happy to oblige, flexing his muscles, cracking his knuckles, entertaining us with braggadocio.

We waited, my stomach grumbled, and the clock ticked on into the afternoon. About 2 o'clock, the door opened and the short man signaled to the Latino with the gold jewelry, "You, you're first."

I lit the last of my cigarettes, opened and read my resume over again for the 30th time.

The thug had a weapon in his pocket, or so he said.

"You mean you guys don't carry a piece?" he asked. "I wouldn't come around this part of town without a piece."

"A piece of what?" the woman asked.

"A gun. A pistola. An argument-stopper," he said.

The door opened a crack; the Latino man was ready to come out, but he was still conversing with the men inside, in Spanish. As he left, he was laughing and did not look at us at all.

The shorter man signaled for the woman to enter and her husband followed her in.

"Not you, her," he was told, but the husband pushed his way into the office saying, "She doesn't go anywhere without me."

The thug asked us: "You guys have your cards, right?"

What cards?

"Your union cards. The guild. Screen actors." He looked at this cluster of pathetic amateurs and shook his head in disgust. "Well, lotsa luck!"

Twenty minutes later, they emerged, the woman looking flummoxed. "Can you believe that man wanted me to take my clothes off?" she said to us.

"He wanted you to strip in his office?" the college student asked in alarm.

"No, not in there! In his movie!" she said. "He said I was perfect for doing the dance of the seven veils. Can you believe that?"

"I told him no way," said the husband. "If she dances, she dances with clothes on. Period." We listened to them talk their way down the stairs and out the door. "Well, maybe I could wear a flesh-colored leotard or something..."

The thug went in next. We heard loud laughter from inside, and when he came out he yelled back to the men inside: "Thursday morning, right? See you then!" As he left, he said to us, "Have a nice life, guys!"

It was after 4 o'clock before I was let in. I sat in a metal folding chair in front of a desk and handed my resume, damp from my perspiring hands, to the man I had been told was the great director, Jackie Hernandez. He was tall and sixtyish with sallow skin, a thin mustache and enormous ears, from which sprouted wiry black hairs.

"Plays, huh?" he mumbled as he glanced at the paper." "Lotsa plays." He tossed the resume aside, leaned back in his chair and looked me in the eye. "You ever ride a horse?"

"Yes, I've ridden horses all my life," I said, and a series of bad and frightening experiences on horseback flashed through my brain. True, I'd taken horseback riding lessons for awhile as a child and had been on horses at Boy Scout camp and a few times more recently, but the horses never seemed to like me and would inevitably try to bite me, buck me or rub me off on a tree.

"You look like a cowboy," the director said to me in his thick, Cuban accent. "You might look good on a horse."

"We make movies for the drive-in," he continued. "These days, they like movies with a lot of sex. That girl," he said, smiling, pointing to the hallway, "she would be good in my movie, but I don't think she will show her skin. What do you think?"

I didn't know what to say; was he asking me about being a cowboy or showing skin?

"You give me your number kid. I call you when I do a cowboy movie."

The short man opened the door for me. I nodded goodbye to the other two losers and left the building, stepping into long shadows

stretching across the parched street. I imagined myself in a Western. A
Marty Robbins tune played in my head:

> *Out in the west Texas town of El Paso,*
> *I fell in love with a Mexican girl…*

The great film director Jackie Hernandez never called. I was neither
surprised nor disappointed. I wasn't about to show my skin, either, or
get into another disagreement with a horse in some soft-porn movie
made for the drive-in.

I found out later that the man who had interviewed me and thought
I'd look good on a horse had nothing to do with "The Old Man and
the Sea," at least not the 1959 version staring Spencer Tracy. That film
was directed by John Sturges, who did some cowboy movies as well,
like "The Magnificent Seven" and "Gunfight at the OK Corral." If
Hernandez did "Old Man," it must have been some Cuban version.

My draft board didn't call, either. They had their shot at me
and waited too long, and before we knew it, Congress had passed a
moratorium on conscription.

I abandoned my ambition to be an actor and went back to the
original plan: finding a job as a teacher. When that failed, I took
the first thing that came along, which was working for a newspaper.
That was 36 years ago, and I'm still working for a newspaper today.
I have not uttered a scripted line or set foot on a stage since 1971,
not counting the few times I volunteered to be the pronouncer at the
county spelling bee.

As for some of the other characters mentioned in this series…
I could Google only one mention of Hylkia de Greve and deduct

only that she is employed by the state government of Victoria, Australia.

Peter Skutches left W&J College not long after I did and moved to England. He returned to the U.S. sometime in the 1980s and has apparently worked as a book editor and writer. "Remembering Malcolm," by Benjamin Karim, with Peters Skutches and David Gallen, a remembrance of black leader Malcolm X, was published in 1996.

As for Ronald Emery, I learned from the Darrow alumni magazine that he and his mother are both living in a retirement home near Utica, N.Y. He suffered a stroke a few years ago and now uses a wheelchair. An alumnus called him recently and spoke to him at length. The alumnus recalled Ron as a man of "refined sensibilities," and noted that Ron "still knows how to soar."

Much of my education occurred in the theater. One thing I learned, with apologies to the Bard for this joke, was that all the stage is a world, and all it players people.

But most of all what I learned to do was to soar, and I have all my fellow cast members, directors and teachers to thank for that.

RICHARD GOLDSBOROUGH, RIGHT, AND I
POSED FOR THIS PHOTO IN OSSINING, N.Y.,
IN MARCH 1969. HE WOULD MOVE INTO MY
APARTMENT IN WASHINGTON, PA., THAT JUNE.

CHAPTER SIX

How to Break an Ankle

Bones, even those of a healthy 20-year-old, will break when stressed in just the right way. This usually happens when you least expect it, so I learned in the summer of 1969. Let me take you back there.

Think back to when you listened to Neil Diamond singing "Sweet Caroline," and Creedence Clearwater Revival doing "Bad Moon Rising." Think about the first time you might have heard "Hot Fun in the Summertime" on the radio. That was the summer of 1969.

My academic performance during my sophomore year at W&J College had been miserable, and so I was forced to attend the summer session to soak up some Shakespeare and sociology. Classes were over at the end of July, and I had the whole month of August to kill before the fall semester began. I had no desire to go home; my parents had moved during the school year to Florida, which was hot and friendless and no home to me.

Spending August at the apartment on North Avenue I shared with friends was an option, but not a good one. We had fun that summer – skinny-dipping at the No. 4 dam south of town, and the party we hosted at our apartment for the moon walk on July 20 – but there were problems. My friend Richard, from my hometown, had enrolled for summer classes and moved in with me. It was his mother's idea. After breaking up with his girlfriend, he had suffered a mental breakdown. She thought summer school would be a good distraction, and that I could keep a close watch on him. I agreed, not knowing just how far over the edge Richard had gone.

You could see Richard coming from blocks away; he was the one wearing the blaze-orange flight suit and the green rubber boots. When you didn't see him, you'd hear him, wailing away on his electric guitar from his nest on the third floor of our building, littered with empty gin bottles. What he played was mainly distortion and feedback, which sounded like torture and brought neighbors to our door begging us to make him turn down the volume.

We fought about this, and one time he even packed his things in his Mercury Cougar and left town, much to my relief. But a few hours later, he returned, promising to behave better. He settled into his nest and, eventually, his old habits returned and he showed no intention of leaving until September.

And so I had to go. I thought I would make it an adventure, so one morning I packed a knapsack, wrote the word WEST on a piece of shirt cardboard with a Magic Marker and left Washington, intending to hitchhike to California.

At 20, I hadn't been alive long enough to acquire much wisdom, which you could see by looking at my feet. I stood at the entrance ramp to the Turnpike in Beaver County wearing a pair of bedroom slippers. They were soft-soled moccasins that I bought at K-mart for $2.99. They were a lot cheaper than real shoes, but they didn't hold up too well on pavement. I'd just buy another pair every time the soles wore through to my bare feet. They looked cool, I thought.

I wouldn't even consider picking up a hitchhiker today, but hitching rides was a common and relatively safe form of transportation for young people in the 1960s. A tractor hauling a flat-bed trailer loaded with girders slowed and stopped and I had to climb like a monkey to get up into the cab. As safe as hitchhiking seemed, you still had to wonder about the people who picked you up. It was always a good idea to take a good look inside the vehicle before you sat down and slammed the door. The truck looked OK: an aqua-colored transistor radio hanging from the roof of the cab, a box of Tiparillos and a statue of the Virgin Mary on the dashboard. The driver, a fortyish, paunchy, jovial man in wifebeater T-shirt, asked me where I was headed.

"California, eventually, but Perrysburg, Ohio, to start," I told him. I planned to mooch off friends first. He said he was headed for Michigan but could drop me off at an exit about 14 miles from my destination. No problem, I thought.

He told me he liked to offer rides, that talking helped keep him awake on the long hauls. He did most of the talking, telling jokes and laughing in that way that some people do – silently, squinting, lips pursed, convulsing. He told me that I couldn't imagine what he witnessed from his seat high above the other cars. He had seen both men and women driving on the turnpike stark naked. He described the sexual acts he had witnessed in passing cars.

We drove west through the hottest and brightest part of that August day with the windows open, bouncing as if we were riding in a stagecoach. Approaching Toledo, he pulled off the road at a place near where I'd be able to get a ride toward Perrysburg. We shook hands, he wished me luck getting to California, I thanked him, opened the door and, forgetting I was about eight feet off the ground, tumbled to the gravel.

But I did not break my ankle then. That would come later.

That the two-lane road to Perrysburg was 14 miles long, and because no one would stop to give me a ride, I had to walk all the way, in my slippers. Dusk and I reached Second Street at the same time, and I was hot, tired, footsore and discouraged.

A quiet had settled on the town; the birds had quit singing, and only the faint humming or air conditioners and the occasional creaking and slamming of a screen door could be heard.

Earlier, walking backward with my thumb stuck out, I had daydreamed of walking into town quite differently: My friends would come running out of their houses, yelling "He's here! By God, he made it!" Their sisters would throw their arms around my neck and peck me with kisses, and we would all march arm in arm to some beer bash held in my honor.

The blue light of television sets flickered and smells of finished suppers emanated from the old houses shaded by sycamores as I reached my friend Monroe's house and knocked on the door.

Monroe and I lived on the same floor of our dormitory our freshman year at W&J. He, his roommate Fred and I became close friends, but both of them left college after that first year, Fred flunking out and Monroe on his own accord. Monroe had the look of British entitlement about him – powder-blue eyes, ruddy cheeks, prominent teeth. Put him in a pair of jodhpurs and riding boots and you'd swear he was one of Queen Elizabeth's sons. He was funny, and kind, and although it never dawned on us at the time, gay. "Gay" was not a term in use at that time. If anyone had ever broached the subject – and no one did – we would have said, "Are you kidding? Monroe's not a homo! He's just… sensitive." We were in denial, despite all the obvious clues. Fred let Monroe do all the decorating in their room, which had posters of Dionne Warwick and Barbra Streisand on the walls, a beaded curtain in the doorway and Judy Garland on the stereo.

I knocked again at the door, but the house was dark and silent.

FRED AND MONROE KILL TIME IN MY
DORM ROOM AT WASHINGTON & JEFFERSON
COLLEGE IN THE FALL OF 1967.

With a heavy sigh, I lifted my pack and padded down the walk toward town, in search of a pay phone and, I hoped, an offer of a bed for the night from one of my other Perrysburg friends.

Monroe was not the only Perrysburg boy to attend W&J College. Regis was also in our class, and through the two of them and visits to their homes on weekends and vacations, I made other friends in the town I thought of as ideal and dreamlike.

It seemed that most times we approached Perrysburg through thunderstorms on the Ohio Turnpike, but in the distance we could see the town gleaming like a diamond, rays of sunlight from a break in the clouds reflecting off wet roofs and church spires. The weather was always perfect in Perrysburg, its people always pleasant, and if there were any problems there, they were packed away in boxes and stacked in cedar closets.

My recollection of those days I spent there in August is foggy after nearly 40 years, but I do remember that I did not see Regis, because he had already left for basic training in the Air Force. And I recall the guilt I felt for my betrayal of him.

In the beginning of our sophomore year at college, Regis and I became close friends and confided in each other about our fear of the future. We felt trapped in college, needing to be there for the draft deferment only. If we left college, we'd be drafted, and there looked to be no end to the Vietnam War, so once we graduated, we'd be sure to be plucked. The U.S. was drafting more than 300,000 young men a year at the time, and although only a small percentage of them would end up in combat, you couldn't tell us that at the time. In our troubled minds, being in the military was equal to death in a rice paddy.

We were angry at the government for the theft of our freedom, torn by the conflict between our own morality and sense of duty to country, and ashamed of our cowardice. So, we made a plan to escape, to emigrate to Australia. At the end of the semester, we withdrew from W&J. I called home and told them that I had quit college, but not about Australia. The next day, my father flew up from Florida, and he, along with Frederick Frank, the dean of students, managed to talk some sense into me, and I re-enrolled.

Regis' father did not come. "I knew you wouldn't go through with it," he told me in disgust as he left for home. Rather than be drafted into the Army, he enlisted in the Air Force. Monroe would do the same.

Regis' family lived on Front Street, and I stopped by to see them. They tried to be pleasant and welcoming, but there was a noticeable chill in the conversation, and awkward avoidance of Regis' name. He was gone, and they could not put aside the fact that I was a cause of that.

When I left their house it started to rain, and it rained all night. I decided it was time to move on.

The drivers of cars and trucks coming through the Ohio Turnpike entrance stopped and grabbed their tickets, then headed up the westbound ramp, their stares fixed straight ahead, ignoring me as I sat on a guardrail holding my "WEST" sign. Patience, I kept reminding myself.

Another group of hitchhikers had appeared beside the eastbound ramp – two girls and a boy, maybe my age or a little younger. Every time a likely looking ride passed them, the girls would jump up and down and wave their signs, like cheerleaders at a fundraiser car wash. One of the signs read "N.Y." and the other said "Woodstock" and was adorned with a guitar and flower crudely drawn with crayon.

I watched them wear themselves out for about half an hour, and then one of the girls crossed the traffic and headed in my direction. She was wearing hip-hugger bellbottoms and a fringed leather vest with nothing on underneath it.

"Hey, man, like where are you going?" she asked me.

I held up my sign and told her California.

"Wow! That's like really far away. What's happening there?"

I told her I didn't know of anything happening there, I just wanted to go there.

"Far out! We're going to the Woodstock Musical Festival. Did you hear about it? Like everyone is going to be there."

I'd heard something about it, but wasn't interested. I had grown up around New York and had gone to boarding school upstate, and I had no desire to be back there at the moment.

"Hey, man, why don't you come with us? It would be groovy."

No thanks, I told her. Wherever she was going, this Woodstock thing, couldn't be as thrilling as California. Of course, I didn't mention that I wasn't going to San Francisco to drop acid and demonstrate against the war and have my fill of free love, but rather going to San Diego to stay with my grandmother, aunts and uncles and share the bedrooms of my juvenile cousins.

"Well, peace, man," she said, flashing me the hand sign before heading back across the ramps. Even before she reached her friends, a VW microbus loaded with luggage on top had stopped to offer them a ride. Pulling away in a sputtering cloud of exhaust, the girl flashed me another peace sign out the window, and I felt a pang of regret.

Trotting after the white Chrysler that had stopped on the ramp, I could see three men in the car. The back door swung open. I took a quick look at what seemed like an episode of "Ozzie and Harriet."

OK, for all of you not old enough to get that, I'm not talking about zoned-out rock and reality star Ozzie Osborne, but rather Ozzie Nelson. That old TV show featured the real-life Nelson family in make-believe situation comedy. The two boys, Ricky and David, were the handsome, athletic, respectful, white-bread ideal sons with no nonsense about them. David's fraternity brothers were always dropping by the house for large helpings of milk and cookies. It was a show about typical America that exists only in the wishful thinking of chuckleheads.

Well anyway, David's fraternity brothers were offering me a ride, which I took. The guy sitting next to me in the back seat was wearing a short-sleeve madras shirt, white jeans with neatly ironed creases, and Docksiders. They all looked as if they'd just come from a barber shop. Where was I going? Why? Where was I from? What did my father do for a living? Did I enjoy sailing? They peppered me with questions, and all three, even the driver, felt compelled to look at me and make eye contact when he spoke. It made me nervous.

"Do you smoke pot?" the one in the back seat, the youngest, asked me. He seemed fascinated with my clothes and long hair and sideburns. I realized that they had picked me up out of curiosity. They had seen hippies before, but they'd never really talked to one. "Sometimes, but I don't make a habit of it." I answered. They all looked very disappointed.

By afternoon we were rolling across industrial Indiana. The questions kept coming: "How long do you think it will take you to get to California?" "Where will you sleep along the way?" "Aren't you afraid of being stranded in the desert?" I hadn't thought about these things, and although I tried to be nonchalant, the questions rang in my head like alarms. I unfolded my map and studied it. Hmmm. I had always thought Iowa was a small state, but on the map it looked enormous, vacant, frightening.

David's fraternity brothers were headed for their homes somewhere north of Chicago. Earlier, I had told them they could drop me off just beyond Gary, Ind. I thought about the 1,750 miles of hot pavement ahead of me and considered the bottoms of my moccasin slippers, purchased just a week earlier but already sprouting holes.

"Do you guys pass O'Hare Airport on your way home?" I asked them. They would. "Then, how about just letting me off there."

Back in 1969, the airlines offered student discounts, and you could fly standby for half price. I used to fly to New York from Pittsburgh for $12, and that included a meal and a complimentary cocktail. So, flying from Chicago to California, rather than hitchhiking, was a no-brainer. I probably paid no more than $40 for the flight to Los Angeles and the connection to San Diego.

I called Bim from the airport in Los Angeles and told him when I would be arriving. Bim was my father's half-brother, just eight years my senior. As a child, visiting relatives in California with my family, I had idolized Bim, the rollicking teenager with a stack of comic books in his closet as high as my head.

Back then, the entire clan would come out to the airport in San Diego to greet us – all my father's siblings and cousins and all of their children – cheering us as we emerged from the baggage area as if we were movie stars. Coming in for a landing, I wondered if I would get the traditional welcome, even on such short notice. But only Bim was waiting for me. I saw him before he saw me, touching up his neatly coifed hair with a pocket comb, standing in the bright sunlight in a white dress shirt and black slacks, looking so adult.

And then he saw me sauntering toward him in an old work shirt and bell-bottoms I had altered myself by slitting the legs and sewing in triangles of bandana cloth, a knapsack flung over my shoulder, the long hair and muttonchops, the aviator sunglasses. Then he recognized me, although his face was screwed into a question mark. He said my name, but it was a question. We shook hands, and he tentatively touched my shoulder. He could not mask his disappointment.

"Jeez! Look at you," he said. "You got so tall, and… I just didn't expect… I mean, what's with the costume?"

He had expected me to appear clean-shaven and clean-cut, dressed appropriately for travel, a younger version of my father, the brother he idolized. I was a shock, from which he would recover, but he would spend the next week or so trying hard to make me "normal."

Bim and his wife, Jeanine, had three little boys, the oldest of which was 9. Perhaps it was for their sake, because my presence would be an influence on them, that Bim was determined to make a man out of me.

My hair wasn't all that long at the time, but it was long enough to make my aunt and uncle worry that I might be one of those kind, you know, "light in the loafers," as he would say, a Nancy-boy. So the first thing they did was to arrange a blind date.

"But I already have a girlfriend," I pleaded, but they ignored this as imaginary nonsense and summoned one Debbie, a neighbor girl who stood about six feet-two in flat shoes, and add another four or five inches for the teased hairdo. I kept this photo of us, in the backyard of Bim's house with my cousins and their dog. Jeanine had sent it to me and had written some quotations on the back. Apparently, I had said, "Boy, are you tall!" And apparently, Debbie had said, "Don't you have any other shoes?"

I can't recall where we went that night or what we did, but I do

A blind date with Debbie, at Bim's house
in San Diego with two of his sons.

remember the crick in my neck I got from looking up all evening.

Bim's next manly endeavor was to take me to San Diego Stadium to watch the Chargers play and exhibition football game. Our seats were in the top row of the highest section, the steps to which were so steep that it was nearly impossible to carry beers up to them without spilling them. We carried many beers. We cheered with such enthusiasm that the few other people sitting below us in our section found other seats where they could remain dry. The top section of seats was so steep that when after my fifth beer I lost my balance I tumbled forward and landed five rows away.

If you think that there is where I finally broke my ankle, you are wrong. I landed as relaxed as a laundry bag filled with lingerie, and got up laughing like a jackass.

No, I would get my punishment, but it would come later.

Although Bim sold insurance for a living, most of his friends had real-man jobs: policemen, firemen, career Marines. He took me to their weekly poker game for some cigar smoking and whiskey sipping and gambling, although these guys played with nothing but pennies. Sorry, but it's not so impressive when the motorcycle cop in a muscle shirt and flat-top pushes a stack into the pile and says, "I raise ya 15 big ones," and a hush falls across the table, even though he's talking about 15 cents.

It was this group of he-men who taught me to play Indian poker. This came late in the evening, when they had had too much to drink and were acting silly. In Indian poker, everyone gets a card that they hold against their own foreheads so that everyone can see the player's card except that player himself. It's a game that seventh-graders find hilarious; for drill sergeants and San Diego's Finest, it's pathetic.

Bim let me ride his motorcycle around the neighborhood, and he promised that he would borrow a friend's bike and the two of us would ride out into the desert and spend the day. But when Saturday came, his friend did also, and I found myself riding passenger on Bim's bike, which was more than disappointing; it was mortifying, because there is nothing so pointless as being a passenger on a motorcycle. It's like watching someone eat a steak while your jaw is wired shut.

Nevertheless, the day was enjoyable, exploring wilderness which today is probably a housing development or a shopping mall. Bim's friend pointed to a cliff from which a trickle of water fell smashing on the rocks below. He said that he had seen a girl standing at the top of that cliff two weeks earlier, stark naked except for a string of beads around her neck.

For a 20-year-old, in 1969, that was an exciting thought. I kept my eyes peeled for naked women, but we saw almost no one the whole day. Exploring around the base of that cliff that afternoon, I found a bead necklace among the wet rocks and put it in my pocket. Years later, I would take that necklace out of a box of mementos and recall that vision of unclothed beauty, that vision that I never experienced other than in a tale told under the canopy of tall aspens on a hot Southern California day.

My mother's family history is simple and straightforward: They came to this country in the early 20th century from Poland, where my mother's parents were born, peasants, like countless generations before them.

My father's family tree is more complicated and mysterious, its trunk and lower branches obscured in the ground fog of time. What little we know about the paternal line is something we'd rather not know at all. You wouldn't either if you found out Booker T. Washington was a slave on your ancestor's Virginia plantation. While Booker T. was working for The Man – James Burroughs – my

Echo Apartment Hotel

1315 13th St. (13th and A), San Diego 2, Calif.
Phone : BElmont 2-9422
22 furnished apts. and 5 hotel rooms, all with
tile baths. Daily, weekly or monthly rates include
linens, utilities, automatic washers and dryers.

Alice —

This post card is
free ! So are the
thousands of beautiful
women here that are
climbing up my back.

See you soon
and you too Charlotte.

— Heaps of affection

The masked marauder

POST CARD

Alice McClenathan
264 E. Hallam Ave
Washington, Pa.

P16622

Near Balboa Park, U. S. Naval Hospital, Balboa
Stadium, Russ Auditorium and S. D. Junior College.

father's mother's Irish and Scottish ancestors were on the Oregon Trail. They became pioneers in Oregon, Washington and Alaska and seafarers who sailed the China route. At the time my mother's mother was boarding a steamship for America, my paternal great-great-grandmother, Ada Woodruff Anderson, was churning out novels about adventure in the Northwest. Her daughter, Great-grandmother McCully, would become a writer, too, mostly of gardening books and articles. Her daughter – my grandmother Dorothy – never published but was a writer at heart, an avid reader and the composer of great letters. She would have a profound influence on my career, although this would not be apparent until years after that summer of '69 in California.

She lived on Bancroft Street in San Diego at the time, an old, quiet neighborhood, with her second husband, Harry, a retired Navy man. It was a house I still walk through and around in my dreams: a garage stacked with dusty curiosities, a miniature house where Gram did her sewing, a lemon tree, a shuffleboard court, and a garden that Harry was constantly tending and watering.

Gram was pencil thin with a constant and broad smile that made her top-heavy. I remember her, there and when she visited us on the East Coast, as delicate and sophisticated, a cigarette and cocktail balancing in her hands like weights on a scale.

I spent a couple of days at their home that August, poking around the garage, playing golf with Harry, and sitting in the porch swing with Gram, and that's where it happened. No, not the broken ankle, but her influence on me: what she would say that would set my course.

It can be brutally hot in the desert just east of San Diego in August, but

MY GRANDMOTHER, DOROTHY ACHENBACH,
AND MY FATHER ENJOY COCKTAIL HOUR IN
BRONXVILLE, N.Y., IN 1956.

not in town, where the breeze passes over the cool waters of Mission Bay and sways the tall palms on Bancroft Street, and wafts over the dahlias coming into bloom in the front yard and caresses us in the shade of the porch.

We were sitting on the porch swing, Gram and I, in the early afternoon, drinking lemonade and talking about my future.

"So after college, what?" she asked.

"Well, it's not like I have much of a choice. Can I have one of your cigarettes?

"No, dear, I'm counting these."

She was always trying to cut down on smoking, restricting herself to a certain number of smokes per day; either that, or trying to keep people from mooching cigarettes from her. They were Parliaments, in a blue and silver box.

"Well, I suppose I'll be drafted, and then shipped off to Vietnam, and then shipped back in a box," I said, trying to be flippant, even though my post-graduate prospects were scaring me to death.

"Oh, don't think that way," she said, waving her bony hand dismissively. She had been a Navy wife for many years, moving her family all over the country and to Panama and back. She said the military was a vast place, and a good place to accumulate life experience, and if I really wanted to be a writer, I would need lots of that.

"You're so young," she said with that deep, halting laugh of hers. "What have you got to write about?"

She talked about her mother and her grandmother and their writing regimens. And she told me I had to read more if I wanted to become a good writer. "All Quiet on the Western Front" and "A Tree Grows in Brooklyn" were a couple of the books she suggested.

Just the other day, I found in my box of mementos a list she had mailed me later, written in her neat, left-leaning script on an index card, 10 books I should read right away. "The Black Rose" and "Green

Dolphin Street," are among them. Regrettably, I have yet to read any of them. But I will.

"Here, go ahead, have one of my cigarettes," she said. "I'll resume quitting tomorrow." She watched me smoke, smiling contentedly, her head cocked to one side.

Read the good authors and learn from them, but don't pay any attention to what is fashionable and contemporary and novel, she said.

"Write about what you know."

The California clan was large, but no one was my age. All my cousins were younger, all my aunts and uncles older. After a week, they didn't know what to do with me. I was too old to take to Disneyland, too young to take to nightclubs. The novelty of my presence began to wear off.

The whole family got together for a picnic in Balboa Park. There would have been no picnic if it were not for my visit. I decided then to leave the next morning. Feeling ashamed about chickening out and flying from Chicago, I decided to buy a real pair of shoes and hitchhike back east.

The adults were playing canasta at the picnic tables, and I was playing soccer with my cousins, trying to dazzle them with smooth moves and crafty dodges. I would dribble circles around them, and they would fall down, mostly from laughter. But moccasins from Kmart that were actually bedroom slippers were not the best footwear for soccer. I stepped on the ball to bat it backward, my foot slipped off and came down hard on something not my foot, and I heard a snap, a muffled crack like a twig crushed under a boot, and felt a lightning strike up my leg.

I got to my feet and hobbled over to the picnic tables. No, it's OK, just need to catch my breath, I told them. But when I rose, I could not put weight on the leg. I sat, and the ankle swelled.

I left the clinic on crutches with a cast – one of those old-fashioned thick plaster things – from my knee to my toes. The broken bones did not worry me as much as how and when I could leave California. Maybe a cast on my leg would be a good lure for rides, but I kept imagining standing along, say, a remote and lonely stretch of road in northern New Mexico, hungry, thirsty, my hands blistered and underarms raw and chafed from crutches, saying to myself over and over again, "You idiot!"

From the window of the plane I saw the dark shapes of seals dancing on the waves of the bay before we banked and headed into morning sun, bound for Phoenix, then New Orleans. My cast was an obstruction in the aisle over which stewardesses stepped gingerly. Bim had written on it in blue Magic Marker a message to my father: "Sorry we broke your kid, Al."

I was headed to Florida – home, if you could call it that. My parents had moved there only recently, to a house I had seen only once. There was nowhere else to go; it would be weeks before it was possible to walk without crutches or drive a car. My romantic, adventurous quest, my dream of hitchhiking across America and accumulating all those life experiences, which my grandmother said I so sorely lacked, was over. Crashed and burned. I was completely defeated.

As the jet cruised above a rusted, empty, waterless landscape, I foresaw the near future. The wandering son would return, penniless and crippled, to the protective custody of his parents. His mother would tap an angry foot on kitchen linoleum and dab tears from the corners of her eyes, bemoaning her child's tattered clothing and foolish behavior, "gallivanting" around the country instead of toiling at a summer job. His father would deliver him to a barber shop for a "real haircut, not just some damn trim." Lectures.

It was necessary to change planes in New Orleans for a flight to Fort

Lauderdale, and the layover was a long one. A wheelchair awaited me as we disembarked. I protested, but a stewardess cut me short. "Sorry, company rules," she said.

The wheelchair came with an attendant. I can't recall his name; let's say it was James. He was a tall, middle-aged man in blue captain's cap and white, short-sleeved shirt that contrasted sharply with his black-almost-purple skin. He spoke softly and slowly and seldom. Yes suh. No suh. Where can I take you suh?

I had no sense, no experience, no understanding of the South, and I felt embarrassed for James, forced to serve this master, this reckless, scruffy white boy.

He rolled me through the airport, to the toilet, to the newsstand, humming discreetly.

"Can you take me outside?" I asked him.

"Lawd, no suh!" he chuckled. "Why, you be parboiled out der in dis heat."

"Just put me by the window then. You can leave me there. I'll be all right." I wanted to free him of this menial task, emancipate him.

My eyes grew heavy watching planes land. I watched shadows move and lengthen. I dozed.

Sometime late in the afternoon, I awoke to the gentle shake of James' hand upon my shoulder. "C'mon suh, it time for you to go home."

And so it was.

What happened to all of these people?

Richard, the friend who shared my North Avenue apartment and whose melancholic guitar outbursts so upset the neighborhood, married a girl from Johnstown, went on to become a stone mason and fathered three daughters. Hobbled by a fall from a scaffold, he endured constant pain until about 20 years ago, when he took his own life.

Fred, Monroe's affable roommate, after flunking out of W&J went on to school and jobs all around the country but was never able to break free of the gravity of Western Pennsylvania. He died here, at 56, of complications from diabetes.

Monroe served in the Air Force in Vietnam, after which he settled in San Francisco, where he worked as a waiter. "Monroe has decided to become a homosexual," Fred told me at the time. He later moved to New York City, where he now owns two trendy Manhattan restaurants.

Regis also served in the Air Force in Vietnam. I returned to Perrysburg in 1972 to be an usher at his wedding. As far as I know, he's still living in Perrysburg and working in the family business.

Bim, my father's half brother, had a bad heart and didn't know it. He died from a reaction to medications at age 63.

I last saw my paternal grandmother, Dorothy McCully Burroughs Achenbach, in the late 1980s. She and Harry had by then moved from Bancroft Street to a double-wide. When my wife, Alice, and I visited them, Gram was dressed in a neat blue suit, but wore enormous, pink, fuzzy slippers. She was still counting her cigarettes. "We are so old!" she complained. Harry died first, and Gram followed a year later.

My mother lived long enough to see me stop gallivanting around the country and settle down, and to enjoy her first grandchild, but not her second. She died of cancer at age 52.

My father remarried and remains in Florida and in good health. He did indeed drag me to a barber shop in August 1969. It was the last time I entered a barber shop. Because…

…the girlfriend I mentioned when Bim and Jeannine arranged my blind date started cutting my hair. She did such a good job of it that I married her, and she has been cutting my hair ever since.

IN EARLY SEPTEMBER 1969, I MANAGED TO
FLOAT IN MY PARENTS' POOL IN FLORIDA BY
WRAPPING AND TAPING MY PLASTER CAST IN A
PLASTER BAG.

DeLloyd Thompson must have posed for
this photo shortly after learning to
fly in 1910.

CHAPTER SEVEN

Early Bird

A wind whipping the air into a static of snow flurries rattled the windows of the clapboard house at 86 West Beau Street on the morning of Saturday, January 29, 1949. At 11 o'clock, Mary Patterson answered her telephone. It was George Herd, owner of the drug store on Main Street, wondering why his employee had not shown up for work.

Mary, who had rented a room after the death of her husband, told George she would wake her boarder. It was not unusual for the man upstairs to sleep late, because in addition to working at Herd's (and running the poker game in the back room there, or so it was said), he also tended bar at night at the Green Tree on North Main Street, also owned by George.

Mary entered the man's room and found him in bed, apparently dead for several hours. As distressing as this sight was, it did not come as a great shock; her boarder was not in the best of health, walking with a pronounced limp, suffering from the effects of a bad car accident several years earlier and laboring for breath from a bad heart. Still, it was such a shame for him to die alone like that, poor man.

Mary rushed downstairs and called George and told him to come down the street right away. Mr. Thompson had passed away, she said.

Born 60 years earlier just a few miles west of the rented room in Washington where he died, DeLloyd Thompson's sad and quiet demise was in ironic contrast to much of the life he led: flamboyant, daring, adventurous and punctuated by great fame and fortune. An aviation pioneer, he made sensational headlines from coast to coast as he smashed speed an altitude records, and outlived most of his fellow stunt pilots in the early, crazy days of flight. An idol to millions of children and adults alike, he thrilled crowds at air shows and speedways, amassed great wealth, and convinced a nation of the dangers and advantages of air warfare.

His rise was meteoric, and his fall a long glide that ended on a cold and windy January day in a town where his very name once caused shivers of pride. In the great technological rush that was the 20th century, his reputation and fortune would dwindle and his memory would be left by the side of the road.

This is the story of "Dutch" Thompson, the birdman, and the spectacular arc of his life.

Sara Thompson gave birth to her second son on Jan. 21, 1889, at the family's home in Coffey' Crossing, just west of Washington in Buffalo Township. She and her husband, Samuel, named the child David Lloyd Thompson, in honor of her father, Capt. David Haggerty.

The family moved to Kansas when David and older brother Clyde Jackson were still not in school. However, Sara and the boys returned to Washington several years later to live with her father. Sometime while attending Seventh Ward School on Shirls Avenue, David picked up the nickname "Dutch." A little later on, he would abandon his first name and start calling himself DeLloyd.

By the time the Wright brothers achieved the first powered flight at Kitty Hawk, N.C., on Dec. 17, 1903, Dutch was nearing his 15th birthday and already fascinated by the automobile and the speed of these

DeLloyd Thompson, left, and his
brother, Clyde, in 1891.

DeLloyd Thompson is shown behind the
wheel of an Oldsmobile that he drove
from Washington, Pa., to Philadelphia in
18 hours, 15 minutes in November 1909.

new machines. School was not much to his liking, and when David H. Swart opened the first automobile garage in Washington County in 1905, in an old factory building on West Maiden Street in Washington, Dutch went to work for him as an apprentice. Swart went on to become a prominent auto dealer, selling Packards and other makes until his death at 81 in 1947, and his young apprentice, having learned to be a mechanic, graduated to racing autos.

On Nov. 23, 1909, a 20-year-old Thompson drove an Oldsmobile from Washington, Pa., to Philadelphia in 18 hours, 15 minutes. The feat seems unremarkable today, but at the time cars were mechanically unreliable and paved roads almost non-existent. Routes would not even be numbered for another 14 years. Although roads existed along the route of what would later be taken by the Pennsylvania Turnpike, Thompson more than likely headed to Uniontown, then on to Cumberland and Hagerstown, Md., before turning north toward Gettysburg. On his return, he posed proudly in the driver's seat for a photo in front of the Washington Auto garage, then on East Maiden Street.

For Dutch, racing cars on dirt tracks and over rutted roads and fields was not thrilling enough. Orville and Wilbur Wright, and now many other mechanics, were designing flying machines that were more reliable, sturdy and could cover longer distances at higher altitude and greater speed. Thompson saw his future not in front of him but above him, in the clouds.

And so, making what would become the most important decision of his life, in the summer of 1910, DeLloyd Thompson headed west, for St. Louis, to find a man named Walter Brookins.

Walter Brookins grew up in the same Dayton, Ohio, neighborhood as did Orville and Wilbur Wright, and he was taught at school by the Wright brothers' sister Katherine. "Brookie," from the age of 4, began tagging after the brothers, who promised to build him a plane when he grew up.

In 1909, Orville Wright made Brookins his first pupil, and he performed his first solo flight after only two and a half hours of instruction. He flew with the Wrights in exhibitions but soon began making a name for himself. On July 10, 1910, in Atlantic City, N.J., he flew to a height of 6,175 feet, a world record.

At about that time, Brookins, had established his own flying school in St. Louis, Mo., and one of his first students was DeLloyd Thompson, an auto mechanic from Washington, Pa., who, like Brookins, was 21 years old.

Thompson was also a quick learner. He made his first solo in a Wright biplane on Aug. 6, 1910. It must have been at about that time that Dutch had his photograph taken at the controls of the biplane, his tweed cap tuned rakishly backward and his upper lip bare of the mustache that would later be his signature for the remainder of his life. And it was at this time that the Wright company agreed to participate in Washington's Centennial celebration Oct. 3-8 with six consecutive days of flying demonstrations.

On Sept. 22, the Washington Reporter announced: "Wilbur Wright and Ray Knabenshue, the famous aeroplane men, have selected a large tract of ground on the Washington and Canonsburg trolley line as an ideal aviation field, and they believe that with fair weather conditions they will be able to break some records during the six days they will fly. Walter Brookins, the young aviator who has accomplished so many sensational flights during the past few months in Atlantic City, Asbury Park and on other aviation fields, will be one of the star performers at the Washington Centennial."

The next week's papers were peppered with flying firsts, including Brookins' winning of a $10,000 prize for smashing the distance record with a flight of 187 miles. On the day Wilbur Wright and Brookins arrived in town, a local reporter gushed: "Mr. Wright is very unassuming. He is just an ordinary man, of course, and never boasts of his achievements. Mr. Brookins is a very young man, pleasant to talk to and is overflowing with aviation enthusiasm."

The Reporter of Oct. 4 described Brookins' first demonstration: "… as the youth at the levers circled about the field in gigantic figure eights the crowd cheered and applauded. Just before Brookins started on his return to earth the afternoon train of the Pennsylvania railroad passed the aviation field and the engineer appreciating the situation greeted the birdman with a long series of toots from his whistle. Every window of the cars was filled with eager faces watching the conquest of the air."

Whether Dutch Thompson returned with Brookins and Wright to his hometown for its celebration and watched these flights is not clear. In all of the articles that week about the demonstrations, his name is not mentioned. He was still an unknown.

But that was soon to change.

Aeronautical happenings were big news in Washington, particularly in the weeks following the Centennial air show at Arden. Several of those events did not immediately involve DeLloyd Thompson but would have profound effects on his career.

It is likely that Thompson was at Kinloch Park in St. Louis on Oct. 12, 1910, when Col. Theodore Roosevelt decided to hop on a biplane for a ride. Arch Hoxsey, one of Thompson's fellow Wright pilots, assured the former president that he would be completely safe, and Roosevelt delighted the crowd, waving to them from above on his 3-minute jaunt.

Meanwhile, the plane that flew at Arden had been shipped to

Belmont Park, N.Y., for an international air show that would go on through the end of October. It was there, on Oct. 25, that Walter Brookins, in an attempt to break the altitude record, crashed and was slightly injured. Unable to compete for the grand prize, the $10,000 would go to Chicago aviator John B. Moisant for flying around the Statue or Liberty. Moisant shocked reporters, predicting that "within a few years we may expect to fly from America to Europe in aeroplanes, we will soon have metal airships which will fly at the rate of 100 miles an hour."

On Nov. 1, Ralph Johnstone would fly his "baby"Wright roadster to a world record 9,714 feet.

It seemed to an excited public that there was no limit to what these daring birdmen could do, reaching record heights nearly every week. But the higher and faster they went, the greater the peril. Just 17 days after setting the altitude mark, Johnstone, while performing with Brookins and Hoxsey in Denver, died when his damaged aircraft plummeted from 500 feet. His death stunned the nation, but it would become just one in a dismal series.

On Dec. 30, in Los Angeles, Hoxsey coaxed his biplane to 11,474 feet to set the world record. The very next day, trying to top his own feat, Hoxsey's plane fell 7,000 feet, ending his life at age 25.

And on that same day, in New Orleans, Moisant would die in another crash witnessed by thousands of spectators.

Dutch Thompson's day was arriving, by the ghoulish process of elimination.

Chicago's Cicero Flying Field had become the center of American aviation, and in 1911, DeLloyd Thompson was pulled into its vortex. This was where most of the flight instruction and experimentation with aeronautics was taking place, and where a fraternity of fliers was forming. Thompson became close friends with Andrew Drew and Max Lillie, the gregarious Swedish immigrant who began the Lillie Flying Station and School at Cicero, later to become the Lillie-Thompson School.

Dutch Thompson, the long-legged six-footer with an engaging personality, typified the daring and dashing young men attracted to the sport. But the flying fraternity was not restricted to men; the romance and danger drew women like Katherine Stinson and Julia Clark as well.

Thompson was still learning tricks and had yet to compete in an air show when he returned home to Washington in November 1911 to visit his mother and brother, then living on South Lincoln Street. But the visit of the aviator was notable enough to be mentioned in the society columns of the Washington Observer.

The first big Chicago-area aviation meet opened on May 30, 1912, when Thompson flew before a large crowd for the first time. That was the same day that Wilbur Wright died in Dayton, Ohio, of typhoid fever at age 45.

A few days later, Thompson received his Aero Club of America instructor's certificate, and in early July, he was hired as the assistant instructor of the Lillie school. At the September meet, marred by the death of fellow pilot Howard Gill, Thompson was one of the top prize-winners ($995) in events before a throng of more than 100,000 in Chicago's Grant Park. And on Oct. 5, he received his Expert Aviator rating, only the third at Cicero and eighth flier in the country to receive it.

The young auto mechanic from Washington had risen to the top ranks in aviation and did so under the tutelage of Walter Brookins and Max Lillie, who both favored a style that stressed safety first and precision maneuvers. But Dutch Thompson's fame would come from testing the limits of his machines and tempting death, which would claim so many more of his friends and colleagues.

The Lillie Flying School moved down to Kinloch Park in the fall of 1912, and then on to San Antonio, Texas, for the remainder of the winter. There, DeLloyd Thompson showed off for the locals, becoming the first person to fly over their city on Jan. 5. The next day, flying with Andrew Drew, he performed a spectacular spiral dive from 3,500 feet.

On March 16, 1913, the San Antonio Express reported, "Since Lincoln Beachey of Chicago has retired from the aviation game, San Antonio, in DeLloyd Thompson, claims the foremost aviator in the country." The next day, Dutch and Drew staged an exhibition of air "warfare," dropping "bombs" made of bags of flour and staging a dogfight. Later that day, Thompson would receive word of the death of his father in Kansas City.

A couple of weeks later, Max Lillie and Thompson packed the planes on a train and returned to Chicago while Drew remained for a while to cover the Mexican Revolution for the St. Louis Post-Dispatch.

Shortly after Drew returned north, the following news report hit the Cicero fraternity hard:

"Lima, Ohio, June 12 – Andrew Drew, amateur aviator and pupil of Orville Wright, dashed to his death in a blazing aeroplane here tonight as a result of a 'little joy ride.'

"Drew fell 200 feet after being in the air but a short time. Drew shut off his motor and those waiting saw a red tongue of flame shoot from his machine as he fell to his death."

Two months later, while flying over Chicago, the propeller of Thompson's Day Tractor biplane snapped in two, damaging a wing. He was able to save his own life, however, by performing a maneuver he first executed with his late friend Drew. "Spiral Drop of 2,500 Feet Saves Aviator," read the headline in a Chicago newspaper on Aug. 2, 1913.

It would hardly be the last time that Dutch Thompson cheated Death.

This photo from Thompson's own
scrapbook, show a daring maneuver,
probably at Kinlkoch Park, Mo.,
in 1912 or 1913.

Thompson, left, and Max Lillie at
Chicago's Cicero Flying Field in 1913.

Max Lillie designed a massive flying boat meant to carry three passengers, and DeLloyd Thompson had planned to fly it in competition in July 1913, according to Carroll Gray, author of "Cicero Flying Flield." But there were some problems...

Gray quotes flier Otto Timm, who witnessed the test of the WALCO Flying Boat: "...was a large amphibious monoplane finished in fine mahogany with deep leather upholstery. It was extremely heavy and powered with a 50 h.p. engine. A large crowd gathered to see the test flight. Four men were holding onto the fuselage as the engine opened up. When the signal was given to let go, the plane did not move, so the men pushed it and got it started. When they stopped pushing, however, it rolled to a stop. It not only wouldn't fly, it wouldn't even taxi."

Lillie and his good friend and assistant Thompson were busy all summer making passenger flights and giving flying lessons, and then, in December, disaster struck again.

Just before 2 p.m. on Monday, Sept. 15, Max Lillie, performing at an air show in Galesburg, Ill., was flying at 1,000 feet past the grandstand when the right wing of his Lillie-Wright Model B biplane collapsed, and the machine flipped over and fell like a spear into the ground. Lillie's wife was watching in the stands and was heard to cry, "My God, he's dead! He's dead."

An investigation into the crash would reveal that the airplane was poorly maintained and inferior metal parts had been used, a surprise given the climate of safety at Cicero.

Lillie's death must have been particularly hard on Dutch Thompson, who drifted away from the school at the end of the year. He would leave the "safe and sane" instructional aviation behind him and begin an odyssey that would propel him nonstop around the nation and lift him to heights man had never before reached.

In 1913, a Russian pilot performed a loop for the first time. That's when a plane goes into a steep climb and does a backward somersault. Until then, no one had attempted the stunt because of the tremendous force to which the wings would be subjected. A few weeks later, a French pilot successfully looped the loop. The big question here was: Who would be the first U.S. aviator to do it?

"I have been experimenting with this feat and have about made ready to try it," DeLloyd Thompson told a reporter for the Illinois State Register on Oct. 6. "I never have yet completely performed it, but I believe it can be done in a biplane and I am having a machine specially strengthened and prepared for the feat. I hope I can get away with it."

Meanwhile, Lincoln Beachey was thinking the same thoughts. Beachey, unquestionably the most famous American stunt flier, had recently retired, citing the morbid curiosity of the crowds who came to witness the deaths of young pilots. But the loop had gotten to him.

Glenn Curtiss, who at first refused to build a plane strong enough to loop for Beachey, relented. Beachey returned from retirement, and on his first flight in the new plane, misjudged its speed. A wing clipped the top of a tent and the landing gear struck two young women sitting on a shed roof to watch the flight. One of the women died, and Beachey once again quit flying. He could not stay away, however, and on Nov. 25, he completed his first loop.

Thompson would not be the first American to fly upside-down, but he was not about to be outdone. In the first major air show of 1914, on March 25 in Los Angeles' Griffith Park, Thompson made his first loop.

On April 13, he set a world record by making eight loops. And five days later, with female passenger Lillian Biorn onboard, he made the first loop with a passenger.

Lincoln Beachey was still a more familiar household name in America, but Thompson was determined to change that.

On the clear afternoon of Aug. 6, 1914, in Overland Park, Kan., DeLloyd Thompson climbed into his Day-Gyro plane, dressed in a sheepskin suit given to him by the polar explorer, Admiral Robert Peary. He strapped a barometric altimeter to his thigh and began his ascent into the blue sky. When his airplane finally ran out of fuel, a shivering Thompson put the craft into a spiral glide and descended to the field.

The Aero Club of America officially certified that Thompson's altitude had reached 15,256 feet. It smashed the record that Lincoln Beachey had set three years earlier at 11,578 feet. The achievement was noted on the front page of The Reporter, Thompson's hometown newspaper, the following day, but only briefly. Stunt flying, that had so captured the imagination of the public was now pushed aside by the news of the Great War – a war in which air power would come into its own.

Thompson and Beachey both toured the country demonstrating in show after show their high-flying dives and loops. But they noticed that these stunts could be viewed from a distance, making it difficult to sell tickets to their performances. So the two began racing their planes close to the ground against automobiles, Thompson facing off against Joe Briggs and Beachey racing Barney Oldfield, then considered "the fastest man on Earth."

Although a number of pilots could claim to have flown upside-down, the position was but brief, at the top of the loop. Beachey

THOMPSON POSES IN THE SHEEPSKIN SUIT
GIVEN HIM BY ADMIRAL ROBERT PEARY FOR
HIS WORLD-RECORD ALTITUDE FLIGHT
ON AUG. 6, 1914.

wanted to fly upside-down over a distance and had a monoplane with an 80-horsepower engine built specially for the purpose. On March 14, 1915, before a crowd estimated at 250,000 at the Panama-Pacific International Exposition, Beachey pulled the plane into a loop to achieve the inverted position. Realizing that his altitude was too low, he pulled the controls to right the plane. The wings snapped off from the force and the fuselage plunged into San Francisco Bay. An autopsy revealed that the "World's Greatest Aviator" had survived the crash and had died, at age 28, from drowning.

Suddenly, Dutch Thompson was the man to see.

Glamour and mystique enveloped Dutch Thompson, and his popularity grew around the country. His every action and word in public was recorded. When the local dignitaries of Huntington, Ind., greeted him in June 1914, they implored him to come have a drink with them. "No, I never drink when I am in the air," Thompson was quoted in the local paper. "Give me a chocolate ice cream soda."

The newspaper went on to describe the pilot's routine: "He climbed into the narrow, enclosed seat of the bi-plane and strapped himself in. He then strapped an aneroid barometer, an instrument for measuring altitude, to his thigh, where it is in plain view. He turned his cap backward and without placing goggles over his eyes announced that he was ready to commence his flight.

"Just before he gave his final word Thompson extracted a pouch of chewing tobacco and took a huge chew. He said he always chews when in the air."

After Beachey's death, Thompson began a two-year tour of fairgrounds with the great auto racer, Barney Oldfield, in April 1915.

Oldfield, 11 years older than Thompson, had started out racing bicycles in 1894. The cigar-chomping showman became the first man to travel a mile in less than a minute. He and Beachey had performed 35 shows together.

The Thompson-Oldfield spectacles drew tens of thousands to witness a race between the holders of speed records in the air and on the ground. Thompson would never be more famous – except for one night in 1916, when his antics would attract the attention and wonder of none other than the president of the United States.

On the night of April 16, 1916, President Woodrow Wilson, contemplating the war in Europe and the threat from Germany, strolled to the window of his White House office and witnessed a flash of light in the sky. It was the first of a series of explosions that brought traffic to a halt on Pennsylvania Avenue and panicked the residents of Washington, D.C. The explosions continued, and then the sky was alight in a trail of fire above the Washington Monument.

DeLloyd "Dutch" Thompson had just "bombed" Washington.

A group calling itself the "National Security League of America" persuaded Thompson to drop onto 20 American cities imitation bombs that carried this message: "This is a fake bomb – but suppose it contained nitro glycerin – what would you do?" Thompson was intrigued by the project, the object being, "to wake up the country... to the dangers of unpreparedness."

His stunt created a national sensation. His purpose, he said, was "to employ the most effective method of impressing officials and members of Congress and the Senate how absolutely at the mercy of hostile aircraft are the great cities of our country.

"I could have blown the White House and Capitol off the map had I

THOMPSON DISPLAYS THE ALTIMETER HE
USED IN HIS STUNT FLYING.

THIS INTERNATIONAL FILM SERVICE PHOTO
SHOWING THOMSON'S SPIRAL BOMBING
RUN OVER THE WASHINGTON MONUMENT
APPEARED IN THE NEW YORK TRIBUNE
ON APRIL 24, 1916.

been armed with the most deadly explosives, instead of fireworks bombs timed to explode 1,000 feet in the air."

Thompson had been interested in the idea of air warfare ever since two Bulgarians for the first time dropped bombs from a plane on a Turkish railway station in October 1912. It was just a few months later that he and Andrew Drew staged a dogfight and dropped flour bombs during a show in San Antonio, Texas.

The next city to be bombed was New York, two nights later. This time, the War Department was involved in Thompson's plan, having given its blessing for his departure from Governor's Island, even though local officials had not been informed. He dropped five explosive devices, each containing about an ounce of dynamite. The fifth bomb, however, exploded close to the plane and damaged the wing, making it necessary for him to return for an emergency landing.

Thompson bombed Chicago on April 23, in a show that included Ruth Law, the first woman to perform a loop and to fly in darkness. She did two loops over the city that night.

The object of the demonstration, Thompson said, was to alert Congress for the need for as much as $40 million to build an air force and train pilots. But his efforts on the part of national defense would soon be interrupted when his luck came suddenly to a crashing halt.

DeLloyd Thompson enjoyed the company of women, on the ground and above it. It was with Marian Tichner seated in front of him that he broke the air speed record on April 29, 1916, at New York's Hempstead course. His plane traveled a mile in 33.2 seconds, or 108.4 mph.

Five days later, Thompson was seated in the passenger seat of a plane flown by test pilot Harold Blakely from Garden City Aviation field when the craft went into a spin at 600 feet and plummeted toward the ground. The right wing struck the ground first, shattering the heavy wooden frame. The 125-horsepower engine was buried a foot into the earth, and Thompson, riding in the front cockpit, was flung forward, his right leg catching in the passenger seat. Both men survived the crash, by Thompson's leg was broken in two places below the knee and his foot and ankle were badly crushed. He spent weeks in a Manhattan hospital and suffered from blood poisoning and other complications. Despite nearly constant pain, he was back at the controls of a plane while still walking on crutches.

Thompson never really recovered from the crash, however. He walked with a pronounced limp for the rest of his life, but just as importantly, other pilots and aviation technology seemed to pass him as he recuperated.

The United States was soon to enter the war in Europe, and Thompson would have liked nothing better than to fly planes for the military, but his injuries would make that impossible. He would serve as a lieutenant in the reserves, instructing American pilots in the U.S. Army Air Corps, but broken and disheartened, remained in that capacity only briefly. He had reached the apex of his magnificent career and had begun his descent.

The war made heroes of the new young pilots, and the planes they flew were now faster, more powerful and maneuverable than anything Dutch Thompson was flying at fairgrounds before diminishing audiences.

He had accumulated great wealth as a barnstormer, but Thompson would need to find other things to do with his time and money. And he would return home to do that.

On March 29, 1917, DeLloyd Thompson, then in Los Angeles, wrote to his friend, Lawrence Stewart, an editor of the Washington Observer,

DeLLoyd Thompson is shown in the
cockpit of his plane after his last
flying exhibition at his hometown
in 1922.

with a proposal. Thompson wanted to recruit America's greatest automobile drivers, train them to fly, and then form a crack squadron to join the war effort. He had already received commitments from 18 of the top 20 drivers, who would all be assembling in Uniontown, Pa., in May for the first big races of the season.

Thompson wanted to start an aviation school back east, but he needed planes suitable for training. Because both he and Stewart were members of the local Elks lodge, Thompson wondered if the lodge might be able to come up with the $3,000 he would need to build a trainer. He suggested that "Donated by B.P.O.E. Washington, Pa." Could be painted on the machine's wings.

The Elks reacted enthusiastically to the proposal and even offered to raise money for a second plane, but Thompson said that was not necessary because he expected the U.S. government to provide him with one.

Thompson's effort was in response to a complaint the American public had with athletes, celebrities and racecar drivers, about their lack of enthusiasm for the war effort. On April 26, Thompson made headlines by proposing to train in Uniontown the great Australian middleweight boxing champion, Les Darcy, to fly for the U.S. Darcy had left Australia in a controversy over its draft. But a few days later, Darcy, 21, fell ill. He died of pneumonia on May 24.

At the Uniontown races, Dutch Thompson entertained the crowds with a flying exhibition, and on May 9 narrowly escaped a crash when his engine stalled at 3,000 feet.

The U.S. entered the Great War and established the draft. In the tumult to support the war effort, Thompson's flying school never got off the ground.

Griffith Borgeson, in his book, "The Golden Age of the American Racing Car," writes of another scheme Thompson pursued late that year: "After the death of Lincoln Beachey, DeLloyd Thompson became

America's most glamorous aviator and a very wealthy man. He approached (Harry Miller) in 1917 with the proposal that they pool their talents in the development and promotion of a large and powerful military aircraft engine that, if successful, could make them both immensely rich. He offered Miller a check for $50,000 just to get things off the ground, and a partnership was born."

But after they built a 12-cylinder, 500-horsepower engine and gave it a 100-hour test in Daytona, Fla., Miller walked out on the project to pursue other interests.

Faced with another failure, Thompson turned again to his old friends on the car-racing curcuit – Barney Oldfield and Tommy Milton – and starting out in Wheeling, W.Va., returned to the driving thrill of his youth. He would travel around the country for a couple more years, but return home in 1922 and find something that would keep him here for good.

Her name was Naomi.

In 1922, DeLloyd Thompson came home for good and flew his last exhibition at the fairgrounds in Arden. One of those to watch the dashing pilot perform his "undertaker's roll" was a teenage tennis sensation by the name of Naomi Parkinson. The daughter of a prominent local attorney, Naomi had graduated from the Washington Female Seminary and had enrolled at Carnegie Tech.

At 19, Naomi had already racked up a number of amateur tennis championships and had a promising academic future ahead of her, but all that would be put aside when she fell for Dutch. He was 33, and their elopement was scandalous. Their son, Robert, was born in September 1923.

Thompson purchased an interest in a coal mine, and later dabbled in oil wells and took on construction projects as a contractor. He was

NAOMI PARKINSON, THE TEENAGE TENNIS
STAR, ABANDONED COLLEGE AND TENNIS TO
MARRY THE DASHING AVIATOR THOMPSON
IN 1922.

involved in the construction of the Sunset Beach pool near Claysville, which opened in 1926. According to the late Robert Thompson's widow, Margaret, Dutch lost a good bit of money on construction equipment he purchased. "From what I know, he was never much of a businessman," she said.

By the late 1920s, Thompson's wealth was all but gone. He and Naomi were living with his mother, Sarah, in their home at 140 Shirls Avenue, and money problems were beginning to eat away at their relationship. Sarah died just before Christmas 1928. The marriage would dissolve a few years later.

Naomi would pick up single life where she left off. By 1933, she was ranked 19th in the nation among female tennis players. She returned to college in 1937 and made the Carnegie Tech tennis team – the only woman on the squad – and captained the team in 1939. She earned two bachelor's degrees from Tech, one in voice and one in music supervision.

She began teaching music, but when the war began, she joined the Red Cross and served for two years in India, Burma and China.

After the war, she continued to collect trophies for both tennis and golf. She remarried, to Robert Kenward, and died in 1995 at the age of 92. Her life is a story in itself, perhaps for another day. This is, after all, the story of Dutch Thompson, and although his daredevil days were done, he would have one more chance to cheat Death.

Through the worst years of the Great Depression, DeLloyd Thompson was still rich with dreams and schemes. In 1937, he took to the air for the last time, flying the airplane he had designed and built, the Deloyd Cabinaire, from a field in Meadow Lands. Featuring a completely enclosed cabin, the two-seater monoplane was said to be safe and easy to fly and land. But production of the plane ended at two. It was the Depression after all, and the market for leisure aircraft was nil.

Thompson's next venture was not up the air but into politics. Hoping to capitalize on his fame and the familiarity of his name, he filed as a candidate for mayor of the city of Washington in the 1939 Democratic primary. He bought no newspaper advertising and was soundly defeated, placing third with 773 votes. J. Brady Marble won the nomination with 1,756 votes and went on to lose to Republican George Krause in the general election.

The 1940s found Dutch working as a bartender at the Green Tree, a tavern and restaurant in the basement of a building on the east side of North Main Street. His social life, much of it involving gambling, revolved around the Green Tree and his circle of friends that frequented it.

On the night of March 27, 1945, Thompson and three of those friends were on Route 40, headed for Wheeling. Just after midnight, a short distance from the West Virginia line, their car slammed into the back of a truck of the Pittsburgh-Wheeling Warehouse Co. Dutch, who was driving, was the most severely injured, with lacerations to the head and internal injuries. Jack Athens, 45, had a fractured arm and head injuries; Mike Renovich, 51, had head and facial lacerations, and Sherman Rankin, 54, suffered head injuries, lacerations and contusions. These were the days before safety glass and seat belts.

Two days later, the Washington Observer reported Thompson's condition as "poor" and that he had been placed in an oxygen tent. He did recover, but never fully.

After his wife left him, he was not close to his son, Bob, who was shy and so different from his gregarious father. The two would not build a relationship until Bob returned from the war, after serving in Europe with the 81st Airborne and being taken prisoner.

In 1948, an air show at Washington Airport was dedicated in honor

THE DELOYD CABINAIRE WAS JUDGED A
STURDY AND SAFE PRIVATE AIRCRAFT IN 1937,
BUT ONLY TWO WERE PRODUCED.

DeLloyd Thompson ran unsuccessfully
for mayor of Washington in the
1939 Democratic primary, and never
considered politics again.

of Thompson, the aviation pioneer, by Dutch did not even show up for his own party.

That brings us to that cold January morning in 1949, when Mary Patterson went to her boarder's room and found DeLloyd "Dutch" Thompson, once billed as "America's Greatest Aviator," dead in his bed. His business ventures, his marriage and his political ambitions had all ended in failure, and he died alone and broke in a rented room. But all that disappointment was nothing compared to those six glorious years of fame and fortune.

As sad and tragic as his end may seem, Dutch Thompson was not forgotten. In the months following his demise, his friends and admirers came together in an effort to create a fitting memorial to him. And Time would take its toll on it as well.

Two weeks after his death, The Reporter began a drive to raise money for a memorial to DeLloyd Thompson. "…He did as much, or possibly more than any resident of the City to bring honor to this community, as everywhere he went he made certain that people knew he was from Washington and proud of it," read an editorial promoting the fund.

July 13, 1949, was proclaimed DeLloyd Thompson Day by Washington Mayor Elmer Wilson, and more than 5,000 people attended the air show and ceremonies at Washington Airport that day, when memorial gates with bronze plaques honoring Thompson were unveiled and the airport itself dedicated as DeLloyd Thompson Memorial Field. Dignitaries representing the military and the Early Birds, a group of air pioneers that all flew before 1916, were in attendance, as was Col. Roscoe Turner, the great air racer.

"DeLloyd Thompson changed the course of my life when he permitted me to touch his airplane at Memphis, Tenn., in 1914," Turner told the crowd. "I always remembered his kindly attention and during my career tried to be as attentive to other youngsters. You never know when one of your acts will shape the course of some other person."

From the time that Dutch Thompson set the altitude record in 1914 until the end of his life, so much had happened in the development of aircraft. Thompson had lived to see the day when air power decided wars and airplanes flew without propellers. Just 12 years after his death, another local aviator – Joe Walker – would set the altitude record of 169,600 feet, flying the X-15 rocket plane.

The airport grew and went through many changes over the next 20 years, and the memorial gates were abandoned. But in 1969, the plaques were rebronzed and hung in the administration building, and the Washington County Commissioners officially rededicated the airport in honor of Thompson.

The plaques were later removed, however. "I rescued them," Margaret Thompson, widow of the aviator's son, joked. "I think they wanted to melt them down for scrap." She also acquired a wooden propeller from one of Dutch's planes and donated them along with an altimeter, scrapbooks and old photos to the Washington County Historical Society. They are now displayed in the military room at the LeMoyne House.

Few of the pilots who now hang out at the Washington County Airport terminal have even heard of Dutch Thompson, let alone know that it is his memorial field from which they fly. None of those who knew him are still living. His great achievements have disappeared from our consciousness and exist only in piles of yellow, crumbling newspaper clippings. One of those clippings is of an editorial tribute, under the headline, "Aviator 'FliesWest'," written for The Reporter

MARGARET THOMPSON, WIDOW OF DELLOYD
THOMPSON'S SON, ROBERT, IS SHOWN HERE
WITH A DISPLAY OF MEMORABILIA THAT SHE
DONATED TO THE WASHINGTON COUNTY
HISTORICAL SOCIETY.

three days after Thompson's death by Cecil Northrop, once vice president of the newspaper:

"As an old aviator, it is with deep regret that I have been informed of the death of DeLloyd Thompson. His passing removes from the aviation scene one of the very early pioneers of flying, and a most colorful personage in the ever changing development of aviation. 'Dutch' Thompson fortunately lived long enough to see his faith and hope in the future of flying vindicated; and his belief and dream that the ability of man to fly would change the course of men and nations 'in our time.'

"That 'Dutch' derived little, in a material way, for his early courage and daring in the beginning of aviation, is of small consequence, for seldom indeed, have the pioneers in any field in the past died rich men. Without such men, however, this world of ours would be a sorry place in which to live. Intrepid souls, men of vision and courage, ever have paved the way for a great achievement and progress in every field of endeavor."

CHAPTER EIGHT

The Business

"Wake up Maggie I think I got something to say to you
It's late September and I really should be back at school..."
- Rod Stewart, Maggie May

It seemed odd, driving a car in Florida with the windows rolled up, the lyrics of the song on the radio suddenly intelligible, but it was a chilly Sunday morning for November, just cool enough to feel a little homesick for the North.

I had a Styrofoam cup of coffee between my thighs and a pile of newspapers in plastic bags filling the passenger side of my car, headed west, past Dixie Highway, past miles of empty marsh and scrub palm to the new housing projects toward the turnpike. Yes, empty land, because it was 1971, and although Florida was changing rapidly, there were still plenty of places that were quaint, sleepy, and unpeopled. Nowadays, all that marsh and scrub palm west of Fort Lauderdale, Pompano Beach, Deerfield, Delray and Boca Raton is developed to the max, well beyond the turnpike.

My job was to deliver "down routes" and newspapers to customers who called our office and complained that their carrier had missed them or had thrown their paper in a puddle at the end of their driveway. At first I worked four hours a day, seven days a week. Then I went full time. It was not a great job. The customers who called the office were always angry, the pay was miserable. But it was work, and it was not school, which I couldn't stomach any longer; my attempt at graduate studies lasted all of one quarter.

Best of all, I met people, all kinds of people, not just the quirky assortment of souls that worked in the circulation department of the Fort Lauderdale News, but the customers, whose ire often softened when I knocked at their screen doors and surprised them with a fresh newspaper, as late as it might have been.

When I went full time, they sent me out to collect overdue bills. I knocked on the doors of the working poor, the retired folks just scraping by, and lonely people desperate for the company of even bill collectors. No one treated me badly. They often invited me into their homes and out of the sun. They paid what they could. Widows offered me cocktails; others elaborate excuses. I took what I could get, and my boss was delighted.

My boss knew that I planned to be an English teacher, but he kept telling me, "You could go far in this business." I laughed at that at first, but teaching positions seemed nonexistent, and my wife, Alice, and I, newly married, needed money.

Then, one day in December, looking through one of the papers I was delivering, I saw a classified ad that would set the course of my life and thrust me into a cast of extraordinary characters.

The Broward County Sun-Sentinel, the smallish morning daily that shared the same offices and corporate ownership with the much larger evening paper, the Fort Lauderdale News, had advertised for a copy boy. I was, at 23, hardly a boy, and even though the position was even more menial than my delivery job, the prospect of working in the newsroom at the main building downtown excited me. I applied, they hired me, and I stared work there on the second night of 1972.

If there were still copy boys, they would need to be called "copy persons," but that job disappeared along with Linotype machines and the "hot metal" technology that for so long ruled the newspaper industry. A copy boy's purpose was to literally run copy – typed articles and captions and handwritten headlines – from the copy desk in the news room to the composing room, and then run the proofs of those articles back to the copy editors or the proof readers, and then run the proofs back to the composing room. In earlier times, this running was done by actual boys. But by 1972, it was being done by college graduates who needed the work, like me.

Other tasks came my way: making coffee, fetching dinner for the editors at the White Castle, trimming the AP and UPI wires, changing typewriter ribbons, filling glue pots and sharpening pencils. I had to scan what was moving on the wires and keep an ear on the police scanners so that I could keep editors informed of what was going on, down the block and across the globe. To do this, I had to learn what news is, and the man who taught me was Sal.

Sal's wardrobe had been around awhile. My guess is that he'd not had new clothes since the ones his mother bought him while he was in college in the 1950s. He dressed like a chemical engineer: gray flannel pants, worn shiny at the seat, the creases long gone; white short-sleeve shirts with the cuffs rolled up his biceps; string-bean ties; scuffed shoes with frayed laces; a pocket protector holding his Tiparillos; and one of those gray, narrow-brimmed, woven fedoras favored by encyclopedia salesmen and regulars at the race track. He came to work each night wearing that fedora and a gap-toothed grin, his thick eyeglasses, foggy with fingerprints, slipping down the bridge of his small nose.

Sal was the copy desk chief and my mentor. He taught me about news, and the learning required patience because Sal was a stutterer.

Speaking sentences was so difficult for him that their completion required an exclamation. "Never uh-uh-un-understimate the intelligence of reh-reh-readers!" he would tell me. "They're not st-st-st – ga-goddadamit I can't say it – they're nah-nah-not stupid!"

Sal liked me. I showed up for work early, I did things without being told. I only had to be instructed in tasks one time – much to his relief. But compliments were not his strength. "You're not as dah-dah-dah-dumb as the last kid!" he'd tell me.

Sal's job was to manage the rim, around which sat the copy editors. He's give them the raw wire copy from the various services, tell them how long he wanted the stories to run and what size headline to write. Sal worked for the news editor, who, like everyone else in the newsroom, was also my boss. That was Milt. Sal may have taught me about news, but it was Milt who showed me The Business.

The bell on the Associated Press Teletype machine rang, how many times I don't know because it was so noisy behind the partition where all the wire machines were running. It was just after 4 p.m. on a Monday afternoon in May, and I was hustling to get the wire copy cut and sorted for the editors, who were just filing in for work. They'd told me about the bells, but I had never heard them.

"BULLETIN," the machine punched into the thick ivory-colored paper. Then, "Wallace was felled by gunfire."

I ripped the paper off the machine and walked around the corner to where Milt was just settling into his seat at the desk. He was talking with the managing editor and I was reluctant to interrupt, but after a few seconds, I did. "Wallace has been shot," I said, handing him the bulletin. There was no doubt who Wallace was – the Alabama governor was running for president and had been gunned down at a campaign stop in Maryland.

"Jesus! Why didn't you scream it?" he yelled, grabbing the paper from my hand and dashing behind the partition. "Wallace is shot!" he yelled over the partition and into the newsroom. "Tell them to hold the Final!"

The Final Edition of the afternoon paper – the Fort Lauderdale News – was about to go to press. The Final was not home-delivered but rather sent out to a few newsstands, where handfuls of old men gathered and awaited it for the results of the horse races or the stock market report.

A dozen people had crammed behind the partition to await the next dispatches. The bell rang on the United Press International machine, but the bulletin that followed was vague, only stating that shots had been fired at the campaign rally.

I watched in awe as Milt took charge of the situation, barking out orders to the city editor, even the managing editor, about what angles he wanted to be covered and who should be called for reaction. He demanded extra news space in the paper, even if it meant killing advertisements; he shouted into the telephone for later deadlines and an increased press run. I was beginning to realize that the news business wasn't just about getting the news and printing it; it was about getting the truth, the whole story, and getting it first, and getting it out fast, to as many readers as possible, even to people who might never have read the newspaper before.

Later that night, when things had calmed down a little, Milt slapped me on the back, kneaded my shoulder and said softly for my ears only: "Next time you hear that bell ring, you yell like your hand was slammed in a car door, you understand?"

Many years later, someone told me Milt had once worked as a reporter in Birmingham and had actually known Gov. Wallace. It might seem strange that he never mentioned it at the time, but then that was Milt, and Milt was all business, as I learned.

When Milt walked into the newsroom, people who were gabbing or laughing or horsing around always quieted and got down to work. He was a tall man in his early 40s, clean-shaven, his dark hair slicked back. If he ever smiled, I don't remember it; his laugh was more of a grunt, or an angry Hah!

He liked to talk baseball with Sal, who was a fan of the new expansion team, the Houston Astros, but beyond that, all was business. He was an attentive and demanding boss. One night, he caught me doodling while I was on hold on the telephone. But he liked what he saw and asked me to draw an illustration – more of a cartoon – to accompany a front-page story. After that, he and Sal would order me to draw illustrations, which I didn't mind, except that I had many other things they wanted me to do just as much, like compiling the TV listings and the club and church news. I would take on anything they gave me, because I wanted to prove I was worth more than what they were paying me, which was, after taxes, just $59 a week.

But I had a problem: I couldn't type. I didn't dare tell them that; how could I expect them to ever let me attempt to write a news story if they knew I couldn't type? So, what I did was take the TV information and all the releases we got from clubs and churches and the military home with me, and I would start in the morning typing them up in my hunt-and-peck style and often finish them just before it was time to go to work. They never questioned me about when I found the time to type these things, and eventually my typing became fast enough to do some of the work in the newsroom.

I still had to do all the other copy-boy jobs, like fetching everyone else their dinner. I hated that worse than anything, because the cheeseburgers and fries and fish sandwiches and BLTs smelled so good,

"… I COULDN'T TYPE. I DIDN'T DARE TELL
THEM THAT… SO, WHAT I DID WAS TAKE THE
TV INFORMATION AND ALL THE RELEASES WE
GOT FROM CLUBS AND CHURCHES AND THE
MILITARY HOME WITH ME, AND I WOULD START
IN THE MORNING TYPING THEM UP IN MY HUNT-
AND-PECK STYLE AND OFTEN FINISH THEM JUST
BEFORE IT WAS TIME TO GO TO WORK."

and I couldn't afford to eat like that. Most nights, my supper consisted of a tiny can of Dinty Moore beef stew purchased at a vending machine in the company lunchroom.

My dinner breaks were rarely more than 20 minutes, and even then I'd be greeted by Sal upon my return to the newsroom with, "Wah-wah-wah-where the he-he-hell ya been?!"

I began to feel resentful about being everyone's go-fer, and eventually the bitterness would cause me to leave the Sun-Sentinel, but not before I was taught a few more life lessons.

The copy editors who worked on "the rim" at the Sun-Sentinel were an odd collection of silent loners. Most had worked at half a dozen newspapers over the course of their careers, drifting from city to city, finding work that really never varied, no matter what newspaper employed them. Give one of them a glue pot, a pica ruler and a pair of scissors, and he could pick up where he left off a week earlier in Dallas or Atlanta. When a marriage soured or a gambling debt couldn't be paid, he moved on to another town, and another drifter would be hired to replace him.

One of the deskmen was a skinny, acne-scarred guy with a drawer full of axes to grind, a temperamental perfectionist. He wore long-sleeved white shirts, the cuffs and sleeves of which were permanently stained by printer's ink and pencil dust. Another was a small man in his early 70s who wore a bow tie, suspenders and a green eyeshade every day. And then there was Roy, fiftyish, shy and affable, with wavy brown hair, a puffy face and a bulbous red nose. He rarely spoke and worked intently, quietly humming a Bach fugue or a Mozart concerto. He had an intellectual air about him; one might easily presume him to be a college professor or an Irish poet.

One night, Roy didn't show up for work. Milt was off on a short vacation and wasn't there either, which was a relief to everyone who knew how crabby Milt could be when someone called off sick. Milt returned two nights later, but Roy hadn't. Milt was furious and took it out on Sal. "Did you call his apartment? Did you call his sister?" he demanded of Sal. "Did you go to his apartment? My God, he could be lying there dead!"

"Wah-wah-went there!" Sal said. "Landlord sah-said he, he, he left!"

"I was afraid this would happen," Milt said, collecting himself, returning to his seat and the work that awaited him.

A few hours later, we heard a commotion in the hall, and then Roy burst into the newsroom, flushed, his forehead beaded with sweat, his shirttail hanging out, his eyes wide but bleary. "Oh, Milt!" he blubbered, stumbling in his direction. "It's incredible, the most incredible thing! I'm so sorry, so sorry."

The rest of us in the newsroom seemed to suck in our breath in unison, waiting for what we thought would be Milt's explosion of rage. But nothing of the kind occurred.

"Are you all right, Roy?" Milt asked him, curling his arm around his shoulder. "You haven't done anything stupid, now have you?"

"No, I just want to come back to work, Milt, won't you let me do that? I didn't do anything stupid this time, I promise."

"First, let's go have a cup of coffee somewhere, OK?" Milt said gently. "You, me and Sal."

Milt and Sal retuned around 8 o'clock, without Roy, and resumed their work without comment. Later, I heard Milt go over to Cindy at the city desk and tell her, "Roy's done. Son of a bitch. We worked together in Birmingham. I brought him here from New Orleans. He's one hell of a newsman, but that's one sad case, I tell you."

Cindy was a tough woman, but not that tough. She stabbed at the tears in the corners of her eyes with a Kleenex. "Roy's an alcoholic," she explained to me later. You see a lot of that in this business."

And Cindy would know, having wrestled with that same demon herself.

Summer had come to southern Florida, not that we could detect any change in the weather. By mid-morning the air became sweltering. I had to take a spare shirt to change into once I arrived at work in my car that had no air-conditioner. Every day at about 4 o'clock, a torrential downpour would bring a little relief from the heat and gave our photographers something to do.

Cindy would look over the prints that landed on her desk and laugh derisively. It was the same thing, every day. She could count on a photo of a car plowing through six inches of water on a street in downtown Fort Lauderdale, and another of Margate ducks cavorting in a lake-like puddle created by the thunderstorm.

"Duck art!" she'd complain. "Can't I have anything to fill these pages with except this damned duck art?"

Downtown Fort Lauderdale was an odd place at the time. It's tall office buildings had risen out of nowhere only a decade earlier, but already it was abandoned, the shoppers having left for the big new malls. Merchants turned on the lights in their dusty shops only when customers entered. It took me 30 minutes to drive downtown from our home in Lighthouse Point – a distance of about six miles – because of the heavy traffic on U.S. 1. Alice had it worse, however; she had to commute to Miami - 90 minutes each way, much of it bumper to bumper.

We were getting tired of Florida, which seemed a good place for singles and the retired but an awfully tough place to start a career. And we were homesick for the North, where the seasons changed, and with them our spirits.

I still had it in mind to be a teacher, but the newspaper business was becoming more attractive every day. Cindy, short on reporters in a few emergencies, turned to me in desperation. The people I met doing this were different than the ones I shook down for overdue paper bills. I met people with odd hobbies, record holders, politicians and religious cult devotees. I didn't disappoint Cindy, and I started thinking that being a reporter might be a better job than teaching.

But there was a problem – one that I couldn't do anything about, even by working at home. I could never be a reporter at the Sun-Sentinel, no matter how well I wrote or how much I hustled. And even today I can still taste the bitterness from this.

Mr. P, the managing editor, was not as intimidating as Milt. He was that type of man who wears cuff links and never loosens his tie but is always talking about hard work and tough times. His dark tan came from the amount of time he spent on his boat. When he wasn't holding meetings behind his closed office door, Mr. P patrolled the newsroom, picking conversations. He was always the one to laugh the loudest at jokes. Behind his back, some referred to him as a "company man."

I made an appointment to see Mr. P privately. I wanted to tell him that I decided I'd rather be a reporter than and English teacher. He listened to what I had to say, smiling and nodding, and then he said, "That's not possible."

"Why not?" I asked.

"You need at least a bachelor's degree in journalism."

"But I have a degree in English."

"I'm sorry, that's just the company's policy."

"That's not right."

"It may not be right, but it's policy," Mr. P said, rising from his chair to signal the end of conversation. He slapped me on the back as he showed me the door. Steve, the city editor was waiting to see him.

"Steve, don't you think this kid would make a great rewrite man?" he said. "I think that's your future here, kid. I like that idea. Think about that Steve."

Rewrite? Rewrite! That sounded so 1940s. It conjured up images of cigar-chomping press hounds in fedoras rushing for the phone banks at the courthouse, yelling into those antique mouth horns, "Mabel! Get me rewrite!" Criminy! I thought. This was 1972. Typewritten pages could now be placed into a facsimile machine and transmitted over telephone wires thousands of miles away and be received in a matter of minutes. And he's still talking "rewrite"?

The next morning, I started making plans for a trip north to look for teaching jobs. To hell with this stupid business, I thought. I mean, they actually have me take their new reporters around and show them the ropes, and then they tell me my degree isn't good enough? Teaching school couldn't be this bad.

That trip north would indeed change my life's course, but not in the direction I expected.

Between interviews for teaching positions in Maryland and Pennsylvania, I stayed with my wife's parents here in Washington, Pa., where I had spent four years at college. My father-in-law had been talking me up with some of his acquaintances at the local newspaper, and he convinced me to ask them for a meeting.

I arrived at the Observer-Reporter office on a Saturday morning, when the company's board of directors was meeting, and they put aside their business for a while to interview me. Had I taken any journalism courses at W&J College, the publisher asked me. No, I hadn't, and that sinking feeling came over me again. They were skeptical: Why would anyone want to move from Florida to this place?

I returned to my job at the Sun-Sentinel, disheartened at how my interviews had played out. Being a rewrite man was at least better than being everyone's go-fer, I tried to tell myself, but I was bitter, unhappy, and, along with Alice, sick of Florida sunshine.

Then, in July, I received a letter from the publisher of the O-R, offering me a job as a sports writer. Odd, I thought, because we hadn't even mentioned sports during the interview. And odd because I wasn't even much of a sports fan. I wrote back immediately and accepted. I was anxious about returning to Pennsylvania, about taking on a job about which I knew very little, about where I would land once I failed, or succeeded. But this was something I could wave in Mr. P's face. I could thumb my nose at the Sun-Sentinel, its parent company and its stupid policies, at Florida and its ridiculous and monotonous weather. I could set the bridge afire.

On a humid August morning, we left Lighthouse Point, I behind the wheel of the rental truck and Alice and the cat following in the Volkswagen filled with potted plants. The truck seemed to have a top speed of about 45 miles per hour, so it took us three torturous days to reach Pennsylvania. By the time we arrived, Alice's allergies had kicked in and I, having caught a terrible head cold, was half deaf.

When we finally arrived late on a Sunday afternoon, I called my new boss, the sports editor, to let him know I'd gotten there and that we needed to unload the truck and that I'd be in the next day.

"Come in now," Byron told me. "I need you here tonight."

What had I gotten myself into this time?

The Sun-Sentinel was very much a new newspaper, and the Observer-Reporter was the opposite. The Reporter was founded in 1808, and had been an afternoon daily circulating in the city since the middle of the 19th century. The Observer came along later, in 1876, and became a daily morning paper circulating throughout Washington County in 1889. The owner of The Observer bought The Reporter in 1902 and published both of them until 1967, when the papers were merged into the Observer-Reporter, publishing twice daily, in the morning and afternoon.

When I showed up for work for the first time in August 1972, I stepped into a building rich in history, tradition and habit. The desk at which I sat was used by the building's first inhabitants in 1923, I would learn later. My chair, even my waste basket were original equipment, too.

Unlike the huge building in Fort Lauderdale, where the composing room was a 90-second run from the newsroom, this composing room and the deafening staccato of its Linotype machine was on the other side of the wall. The noise of the newsroom – the clattering of wire machines and typewriters, the ringing telephones, the blaring static of police radios, the yelling from desk to desk – was the same as any newsroom, but it was confined to a much cozier space here.

Although the two dailies had been merged five years earlier, each staff was separated by age, loyalty and the clock. The dayside staff was composed of generally older employees of the old Reporter; younger and newer employees were assigned to night side. The "society" department worked during the day; the sports department at night. Almost all of the female employees worked during the day, and the night staff was almost all male. Many readers still referred to the morning edition of the paper as The Observer, and the afternoon, or "Final," as The Reporter. Loyalties of this kind take years to dissolve.

But just as it was in Florida, and perhaps even more, this newspaper office was populated by an intriguing cast of characters: quirky, eccentric, obnoxious, loveable, comic and tragic. Most of them are gone now, but their exploits live on, in memory, and in some cases, legend.

Take, for instance, the man sitting right next to me that first night of work: Fred Sigler.

In December 1957, a staffer for The Reporter – a quiet, humorous intellectual prone to the same kind of absences as Roy was at the Sun-Sentinel – wrote this about a new employee at the newspaper: "Fred is a prolific reader, a walking compendium of sports arcana, supports Pitt when away from home, and is a dangerous opponent in an office pool." A head shot accompanying the article showed a chubby, floppy-eared man in a bow tie.

Fifteen year later, that man sitting next to me was thick-lipped, obese, non-communicative, expressionless and reluctant to make eye contact. His wooden chair squeaked as he rocked back and forth, absently flipping a pencil in one hand as he stared into the space just above his typewriter roll. It would take me years to know him.

Fred was rumored to have a photographic mind. As one story goes, he was making his rounds as a reporter and stopped at the county jail to read the docket. The guards, deciding to have a little fun with him, said sure, he could see the docket, an enormous book with scores of handwritten entries on each page. They opened the book, Fred looked at the page, then they closed the book a couple of seconds later. Click, went the shutter of Fred's brain. He returned to the office and typed all the information that was on the page he was shown.

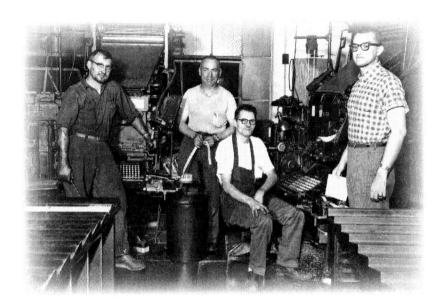

IN THE EARLY 1970S, THE COMPOSING ROOM OF
THE OBSERVER-REPORTER WAS A HOT, NOISY,
DIRTY FACTORY WHERE MOLTEN METAL WAS
FORMED INTO TYPE AND PRESS PLATES.

FRED SIGLER POSES IN THE LIBRARY OF THE
OBSERVER-REPORTER IN 1978.

Fred was famous for his encyclopedic knowledge of sports, which would often earn him complimentary beers at bars and clubs all over town when bets were settled on his authority. Those who knew him in this way were friendly to him, although Fred really had no friends. Those who didn't know him, who had only seen him slowly moving along a street dragging one foot, or rocking on his bar stool, considered him retarded and avoided him.

Fred had difficulty interacting with other humans. He never drove or owned a car, and he spent his vacations following sports teams by bus and train. He lived most of his life in a rented room furnished almost entirely by books. His range of emotion was narrow: bemused contentment, agitation, vacancy. His handwriting was an unintelligible hieroglyphic. He attempted to remove food stains from his shirt with his pencil eraser. In the later years of his life, his health and any sense of hygiene left him. His belly expanded, his teeth loosened, the odor of urine signaled his presence. Even those who bought him beers and pumped him for trivia began to ignore and avoid him.

Fred lived a lonely life and died a lonely death. The Observer-Reporter was his family, his actual relations having abandoned him many years earlier. It's easy now to see that he was autistic; his symptoms were classic. Yet, I doubt any doctor who ever saw Fred came up with that diagnosis. For all of his life, he was simply… odd. It's difficult now to think about Fred Sigler without feeling the ache of regret.

Writing sports was not so much different than writing themes in English class: You seized on a couple of facts you were sure about, and everything else you wrote was B.S. I muddled through the Pony League World Series and the fall season that followed. I was assigned high school football, soccer and cross-country. On Friday nights, we rarely left the newspaper before 2 a.m.

When December arrived, my boss informed me that I was to be the basketball writer. There were just three people in the sports department: Fred, the sports editor and I. Fred answered the phones in the office most nights and the sports editor covered wrestling. This assignment was especially distressing because I knew nothing at all about basketball and had never sat through an entire game of it. No problem, I was told, we'll get someone to teach you the game, sit with you for a game or two.

My incompetence might have gone unnoticed if it were not for the success of the Washington High School boys basketball team, which during my stint in sports would improve itself all the way to the state finals. The team was in the spotlight, and so was my ineptitude.

"As a basketball writer, Park Burroughs, you stink!" someone wrote anonymously in a letter to the editor. I suspect it was a mother of one of the Wash High players. How dead-on right she was!

I like to think that I take criticism well, not ignoring it but rather using the newfound knowledge to my advantage. I might have decided to pour all my effort into becoming a good basketball writer, but I didn't, choosing instead to take the stinging rebuke to heart and follow the letter-writer's advice. I began to plan my escape from the Sports Department.

My desire was to return to hard news, the real world. I would get there, after just two years. Awaiting me there was a whole set of new challenges. The news side was dominated by some unusual personalities – people that my co-workers cautioned me to avoid.

If Charlie asks you to deliver papers to him after work, don't do it, I was warned. Don't get sucked into it, they said.

Charlie was the night editor. He'd take an armload of papers with him to the bars after work and exchange them for drinks. Often, he'd ask one of the young men on the staff to bring him the papers so that he wouldn't have to wait for the press to run and so he could get an early start at drinking. He might buy the staffer a draft beer for the favor.

Charlie used to drink Calvert whiskey and Coke. Then his doctor told him that, because he was diabetic, that drink would kill him. So Charlie switched to Calvert and Tab, a sugar-free mixer. The drink did kill him, eventually.

I avoided Charlie as much as I could, and not just out of fear of becoming his paper boy. He was an ugly man with a bulbous nose who was gruff and humorless and nasty to the proof readers and telephone operator. I can't recall him having anything nice to say about anybody, and no one had anything nice to say about him. His best-known characteristic was his stinginess. He hosted late-night parties at his house but asked his guests to chip in to buy the liquor. Probably the last affair he hosted was the chili party after which he sent bills to his guests for their share of the food and drink.

By the time I went from sports to the news side, Charlie was gone from the newspaper and on his way to the grave. The two younger men who assumed his duties were not at all like Charlie, and I would one day find myself as their assistant.

With Charlie gone, the atmosphere at night was more relaxed. I and a few of the younger guys on the staff, after the paper had been put to bed, would push the desks around on the linoleum floor to clear a space to pitch wadded paper balls at a batter wielding a pica stick or to play broom hockey. Sometimes we would join in the printers' poker game and drink beer and play cards until the not-so-small hours of the morning.

Just about everyone smoked then, and a blue haze of cigarette smoke often hovered in the newsroom. The old Photofax machine printed photos on a continuous roll of chemical-soaked paper. The editors would snip off the roll with a pair of giant copy scissors and pile this paper onto a desk, and the individual photos would be cut apart later, if the pile hadn't been thrown onto an ashtray with a lit cigarette in it. When these piles burst into flames, the standard procedure was to stuff the burning paper in one of the metal waste baskets and pour coffee on it.

But the newsroom during the day was another place entirely. Women worked there, and people behaved accordingly. The proper behavior might well have been enforced by one of those women, a formidable character I will never forget.

The newsroom was a noisy, smoky entranceway to a factory in those days, but one part of it was an island of gentility and neatness, where desktops were decorated with family photos in silver frames, single roses in thin vases, and doilies. This was the Society Department, where Gladys and Charlotte and Ruth worked. They wrote the accounts of weddings, including elaborate descriptions of the bridal gowns. They processed the engagement and birth announcements and chronicled the doings of bridge clubs, charitable organization and Washington's elite. Ruth, a tall, broad-shouldered spinster, a woman who could at one moment be shy or playful, and the next as stern as a 19th-century school marm, was the editor of the society page, authority on etiquette and judge and jury of decorum in the Washington area.

Ruth made rules to which there were no exceptions. Wedding photos would not be used unless received within two weeks of the wedding. "But we can't get our photos back from the photographer that soon!" readers would complain. "But what about our honeymoon?" others asked in appeals to her and the publisher. Sorry, rules are rules.

RUTH RUTHERFORD, WHO CAME INTO THE
BUSINESS AS SPORTS EDITOR DURING WORLD WAR
II, LATER RULED OVER THE SOCIETY DEPARTMENT
FOR 40 YEARS UNTIL HER DEATH IN 1987.

This is a daily newspaper, not a monthly. Even though the "society page" no longer exists, replaced by "lifestyles" and a different attitude about social hierarchy, Ruth's influence is still felt and will be for many years to come.

Ruth was much more than a social maven, though. After graduating from Bethany College, she started working at The Reporter as sports editor, when most of the men were off fighting in the European and Pacific theaters. When they returned, she went to work in the Society Department and stayed there for another 40 years. She was always interested in my family and quick to offer me advice: "You should try writing something for Reader's Digest," she told me and others. She believed that being published in the Digest was the ultimate honor for a young writer.

She had a couple of old cars – old even then in the 1970s: a sporty Triumph TR-3 and an enormous 1958 Buick. I can recall her engaged in lively conversations with her lady friends over lunch and glasses of cabernet at the Union Grill, and I can recall the afternoon when she returned from a doctor's appointment, looking gray and shocked. We knew that she had learned something terrible. A few weeks later, she was in the hospital, and a few weeks after that, she was gone.

Going through her file cabinet after her death in 1987, someone found a pistol, an old six-shooter given to her by Earle Forrest, the late Reporter staffer and historian of Washington County and the Old West. It was the last of many reminders of what a complex woman Ruth Rutherford really was.

About the time I moved over to news side, the Observer-Reporter hired another reporter, a young man who had graduated from Washington & Jefferson College two years after I had. He had no newspaper experience but did have connections: His parents were good friends of the managing editor.

Bob Sturgeon was thin, long-footed and six-feet-four. His long, strawberry-blond hair was already thinning. His face was freckled, and his small chin, wide grin and round cheeks gave him a face that reminded me of Howdy Doody.

Reporting came easy to Bob, but he rushed through every story and had a tendency to be sloppy about details. At a township meeting he covered, a supervisor and a township resident got into a fistfight. He misidentified one of the fighters in his article. The mistake, which damaged the newspaper's credibility and resulted in a front-page apology and a settlement, nearly cost him his job.

He was enthusiastic, whether it be chasing after ambulances and fire trucks or in quaffing gin after work. Often, when we heard word of an armed robbery on the police scanner, we would rush out of the office together and speed to the scene, hoping to interview the robbery victim before the police had a chance to arrive.

We were young and somewhat stupid then and figured that our job should be not just to cover crimes but to solve them. We noticed that over several months, robberies seemed to occur always on Thursdays. So, we began writing about the "Thursday Night Bandit," even though we had little evidence that the same person was responsible.

We all had fun with Bob, at work and afterwards. But he could be as annoying as he was fun. His long hair and his habit of not wearing socks – the preppy style of the time - annoyed many of the older folks in the office. What annoyed me most was his disregard of the truth. He was a habitual liar, someone who not only exaggerated his own accomplishments but invented them entirely. Some people grow out of this, but in Bob's case, it grew worse.

What became really troubling about Bob, however, was the frequency at which, instead of just covering the news, he was becoming a participant in it.

BOB STURGEON JOINED THE STAFF OF THE
OBSERVER-REPORTER IN 1974.

Late one night, while I was assisting on the news desk, we heard
a report on the scanner of a fiery explosion in the northwest part of
the county. We needed to send a reporter, and Bob had already left for
the night. I knew where he was, though – across the street at the bar,
probably burdening someone with his bogus story of meeting John
Lennon at the Mardi Gras in New Orleans, hanging out with him and
writing a song together for which Bob never received credit.

I called the bar and asked for Bob, and I told him to head for the
fire. He was reluctant to leave the bar, but I was insistent. He and a
friend were renting a farmhouse near the reported explosion, so I said,
"C'mon Bob! It's on your way home!"

Bob told us later that he could see the tower of flames from miles away.
The tower became bigger the closer he came to his own house. As it turned
out, an interstate gas line had exploded in his backyard, his roommate had
run for his life, and when Bob came up the driveway as far as the firemen
would allow him, he could see that his house resembled a badly-frosted
cake, the vinyl siding having melted and dripped to the ground.

The cause of the explosion was never determined, although it was
rumored that Bob and his roommate might have had something to do
with it – something Bob vehemently denied.

A large part of a night reporter's job is covering auto accidents. Bob
covered many of them and was the victim, not the writer, of one of
them. Coming back from Pittsburgh one night, he slammed his car into
the divider just before the entrance to the Fort Pitt Tunnels. I visited him
in the hospital a couple of days later. His eyes were blackened and his leg
was in traction with steel rods impaling his knee.

"I'm not as bad off as some of these people are in this hospital,"
he laughed. "Please, if I ever get that sick, just give me a bottle of Jack

Daniel's and a .357 magnum and let me end it in style."

Bob's life would end sooner than he would expect, and when that day came, style would play no part.

Bob's extracurricular activities became wilder and his behavior at work stranger as time went on. He went through a phase when he would tell other people in the newsroom to be quiet because he was trying to meditate. He once flew into a rage after reading an Associated Press story about a drug bust that netted millions of dollars worth of cocaine. "Why do they waste their time on this? Cocaine is not dangerous!" he fumed. "It's a harmless recreation!"

Late one afternoon, the city editor asked me if knew where Bob was. I told him that I'd seen him sitting in his car, parked in front of the building, when I arrived. I was told to go and tell Bob that it was time for him to be at work. His car was an old station wagon, one of those with the fake wooden paneling. I saw Bob sitting in the car with the windows rolled up, his head bobbing, his right hand slapping out a rhythm on the dashboard. I knocked on the passenger side window and Bob signaled for me to get in. The tape player was blasting out a Grateful Dead song and the air inside the car was thick with marijuana smoke. Bob sucked at a joint he was holding with a roach clip, inhaled deeply, and then coughing, offered the clip to me. "No thanks," I said. "It's time to go to work."

"Yeah yeah yeah, I'll be up in a bit," he said, his fingers doing a manic dance across the dashboard as if it were a piano. "Don't you just love this music? There's nothing quite like the Dead. Did I ever tell you about the time I met Jerry Garcia? We were hanging out…" I didn't bother to listen to the rest of the story.

In those days, almost no one was fired from the newspaper, but Bob was coming close. And then one day, much to the relief of his supervisors, he announced that he was quitting. He'd found another job at a newspaper in a neighboring county that published in the afternoon. That meant that he would no longer have to work nights, as the rest of us poor slobs had to.

After he'd gone, Bob kept in touch by telephone, and news of his misadventures came to us through our network of journalists in this part of the state. His life after he left us was a slow-motion fall down a long staircase. Through the years and from a distance, we heard him crashing. We clucked our tongues and shook our heads.

Not long after he left the Observer-Reporter, Bob ended up in a police report again, this time as the victim in a shooting. He'd been back here visiting at his parents home. He told police that he confronted a pair of prowlers in the garage, and one of them picked up a rifle that had been stored in the garage and shot Bob in the shoulder before fleeing, without the gun. Privately, the police told us they thought Bob had shot himself, either accidentally or not, and that the prowlers did not exist.

About a year later, the editor of the paper for which Bob had gone to work told me that Bob failed to show up for work one day and did not call in. When he still hadn't arrived for work the next day and no one answered the phone at his apartment, the editor went to Bob's place and knocked on the door. The absent reporter came to the door in his underwear and explained to his boss that he hadn't been at work because he had suffered a heart attack.

After he lost his position at that newspaper, Bob miraculously landed a job as a press assistant for our local congressman. Every so often, he would call me from Washington, D.C., with one story after another, some of them believable, some not. He told me once that his younger sister – the only other living member of his immediate family at that time – had died. He told me that he had managed to fly from Atlanta to Washington, D.C., with his Berretta pistol in his pocket. In his last call from D.C. before losing his job there, he told me that he was sharing his apartment with an NBC film crew doing a secret investigation. He could barely move around, he said, without stumbling over cables and into cameras and lights.

I began to realize that whether fiction or not, these event were real to Bob. He was not a liar; he was demented.

Bob returned to the Mon Valley for a while and found work for short periods at a couple of small newspapers. His physical as well as his mental health deteriorated, and the last time I spoke to him, he was calling from a hospital bed.

"Dan Rather is here," Bob told me over the telephone. "He's got his 60 Minutes crew here, and they've got me wired up. They're doing a story about me."

A few months later, Bob was dead.

On a frigid Saturday afternoon in January 1991, I attended his memorial service at the Episcopal church in McMurray. He had been cremated on the instructions of his sister, living on the West Coast and obviously not deceased. It was one of those crisp days of cloudless blue sky when the blinding sun is reflected off snow. The priest had already begun his eulogy when I crept in and took a seat toward the back. The six others is the church sat together in one pew, colorful swatches of light streaming from the stained glass falling on their heads and shoulders.

The priest made no pretense of knowing Bob, but summarized his life from the few details provided to him. Yes, he was at one time intelligent, enthusiastic, good-natured and humorous. The last years of his life had been difficult and painful. He said it was only natural for us to feel bewildered at why such a young man – just 40 years old – should be called by the Lord. I was hardly bewildered, knowing how alcohol and drugs had been doing most of the calling.

After the service, in the vestibule, I talked with the other mourners: the roommate, Greg, who had fled the burning farmhouse; Greg's mother; an attorney who was handling the funeral arrangements; and three elderly friends of Bob's deceased parents. I learned a few more details about his death, that the years of abuse had caused his organs to fail, one after another, that he had lost touch with reality months before.

"Bob was a good writer at one time," I heard myself say. My mind was wandering, though, thinking not of this casualty but of all the other good writers in the business, the ones who had succeeded, made something of themselves, corralled their enthusiasm, defeated their demons, pursued Truth and often came close enough to it to bask in its warmth.

"We're going back to the house for drinks," Greg's mother said to me. "Why don't you join us."

Ironic, I thought, on the death of an alcoholic, to be considering a stiff drink in his memory, but appropriate.

Even though I had nothing left to do that day but to watch a hockey game on television, I declined. "I have other business," I lied.

Bob and Fred and Charlie and Ruth are just a few of the storied characters who plied the trade at this venerable old newspaper. Every so often, I stumble upon their photos in the basement archives or serendipitously come across their bylines on articles pasted on crumbling yellow paper, hidden in the dusty file drawers that our young reporters still use for reference. They may be long dead, but they can never leave here.

It's the nature of The Business.

THE PICKASZ FAMILY – FROM LEFT, JANE, AGNES,
EDDIE AND ADAM – POSED FOR THIS PORTRAIT
IN BUTLER, PA., IN 1913, SHORTLY BEFORE ADAM
DIED IN AN INDUSTRIAL ACCIDENT.

CHAPTER NINE

The Accordion Lesson

The Finland, of the Red Star Line out of Antwerp, Belgium, pulled into New York Harbor on the morning of June 7, 1912, just 43 days after the sinking of the Titanic. Among the 1,000 passengers in its steerage were 7-year-old Janina Pickasz, her mother and her brother. When she emerged from Ellis Island, she had a new American name - Jane.

Jane was my grandmother, and the way she told it, her family, on their way to join her father who had been working in the coal mines, was put aboard a train with cardboard signs hanging from their necks reading, "BURGETTSTOWN, PA." That way, if they were lost in a country where they could not speak a word of the language, they could be directed to their destination.

Life in Krasnik, Poland, had been hard, but to Jane, America seemed worse. There was little more food, and even after she learned to speak English, school was a nightmare, bullied and teased as she was for her accent, even by the Italians who could speak no better than she.

In 1913, the family moved to Butler, where her father found work in a factory. A few months later, he died in an accident in that factory, and the family was left destitute.

Agnes – Jane's mother – remarried, however, and the family moved to Connecticut, where Jane would spend the rest of her life. But this is not the end of the story but rather the beginning. The later years of

Jane's life are what I remember, from about the time she earned her U.S. citizenship in 1956 until her death in 1991. This is the story of the end of a life, and lessons learned.

Jane's mother had little need to learn English. Tucked in Polish neighborhoods in Hamden and New Haven, Conn., she might as well have been back in Krasnik or Lublin. But Jane and her brother, Eddie, had become American, if not in citizenship, at least in spirit.

Jane eventually married another Pole from her neighborhood and quickly began raising her own family. Her first daughter, Irene, was born in 1926, and Shirley came a couple years later. But the marriage was doomed, almost from the start. As the nation began to slide into the Great Depression, Jane's husband left her, much to her relief. "He beat me. He beat me almost every day," she would tell me many years later.

Her husband's abandonment was complete. My mother - Irene - saw him only once again in her lifetime: on her wedding day, a quick glance of him at the back of the crowd gathered on Derby Avenue as she and my father departed on their honeymoon in a shower of rice.

Jane's first husband was banished from memory, from photo albums, and so it was with great surprise that I came across this picture in the bottom of a box of old photos I had taken from Jane's house after her death. Somehow, this one photo had escaped destruction. It is of Irene's first birthday on May 24, 1927.

I look at this photo and wonder how, at that time in history when life in this country became so hard, could Jane have managed alone with two young daughters. She would do it, of course, but not on her own.

My mother, Irene, with her parents on her
first birthday, May 24, 1927.

WITH MY GRANDPARENTS, JANE AND ED, IN
THE LIVING ROOM OF THEIR NEW HAVEN
DUPLEX IN 1950.

Jane worked many jobs, but none more grueling than at the Monarch Laundry. But the struggle to raise her young daughters during the Depression eased when she met and later married Edward Rudowicz.

Although the 1930s were years of bread lines and joblessness, they were also the years of the big bands, and Jane's new husband had one of them. He went by the name of Ed Ruell – "Ed Ruell and His Band." He thought the name sounded more continental, more sophisticated, less Polish, even though Ed played the accordion as well as the piano and polkas were a necessary staple of the band's repertoire.

By the time I – Jane's first grandchild - came on the scene, the band's dates were fewer, and Ed spent more of his time as a church organist and a teacher of piano and accordion. My first memories of him and of my grandmother were in the first floor of a duplex they lived in on Derby Avenue, right next to the block building with enormous red letters spelling, "GARAGE OF MONARCH LAUNDRY."

When students came to the home for their piano and accordion lessons, I was told to make myself scarce, to go to the bedroom or kitchen and be silent. That ––made the lessons and the people who came for them all the more intriguing to me, and I managed ways to spy on them. The strangers who came were seeds planted in my fertile imagination. Here, peeking through the crack of a door or from under a table in a darkened corner, my education began. This is where I learned about the other people who inhabited the world.

To this day, I often find myself calling that large white appliance in the kitchen an "ice box." That's what my parents always called the refrigerator, because they didn't have refrigerators when they were growing up.

I can recall the sun-splashed kitchen at the rear of my grandmother Jane's duplex on Derby Avenue and the ice box - oak with brass latches - where food was kept cool by a block of ice delivered by, well, of course, an ice man.

"Shut that door, the ice will melt," I was told, often. My parents had always had a refrigerator in our own home, so the huge ice cube fascinated me.

There was always a big jar of pencils and pens on the kitchen table, where I would sit and draw pictures on sheets of shirt cardboard, glossy white on one side, gray on the other. My parents sat at the table too, smoking and talking with Jane while she cooked. The whole apartment, but especially the kitchen, always smelled of sauerkraut.

"Ma, one leftover hamburger is not enough to make a meatloaf!" my mother would complain. "You're the only woman I know who can make a meatloaf without meat."

The bell rings and Jane says, "That must be Ronnie, let me get the door." I scramble to my spying position, watch this tall, red-headed teenager sit on the piano bench and lift an accordion from its case and hoist it to his knee. It is a huge instrument with a baby-blue abalone finish. Ronnie pops the snaps and the bellows separate. He puts his long arms through the straps and the bellows close with a groan in the key of C. He flexes his fingers, bumpy with warts.

Edward Rudowicz, teacher of piano and accordion, as the sign says in the living-room window, turns on his stool and thumbs through the sheet music on the stand. "Where were we last week?" he mutters to himself. Then, "'Lady of Spain'," he commands. Let me here the first eight bars."

Ronnie keeps time with his foot, and I notice he is wearing white

WITH MY GREAT-GRANDMOTHER, AGNES, IN
NEW HAVEN IN 1953.

high-top Keds. I can't wait to be a teenager, to wear white high-tops, not to be dragged to Buster Brown Shoes for oxfords, not to be dressed in "outfits" with stupid caps. I want to be like Ronnie, warts and all.

It's 1959, and I am 10 years old and now almost as tall as my grandmother, who's about 5 feet tall in her shoes. When she hugs me she smothers me in her huge balloony breasts, and I am at an age now that this repulses me. Her flowered house dress smells of face powder and Listerine.

Jane and Edward are living on the floor of another duplex, this one in East Haven, across the street from a park. Just like on Derby Avenue, there are Italians living upstairs. The upstairs tenants are always Italians and always have a teenage son named Bobby. "Bobby plays basketball," Grandma tells me, as if this were some sort of big deal. "Bobby has a girlfriend," she says. "Bobby's gonna go to college."

I never see Bobby. I wonder if he really exists.

I like girls. I like it when girls come for their piano lessons. This morning there is one about 14 years old in the living room with Grandpa. Through the bedroom keyhole I see that she is wearing a checkered jumper, a blouse with poofy sleeves, white knee socks and well-scuffed saddle shoes, which she crosses under the bench. Her wavy brown hair is pulled back and held by barrettes. She squints at the sheet music and bites her lower lip. "B flat," Grandpa says. "No, no, no! B-flat!" he scolds.

My sister and I are abandoned here for the weekend while our parents visit with friends. Grandma makes us pancakes, but as usual, there is no syrup. "Grape jelly works just as good," Grandma tells us. While she flips our pancakes, Chi-chi, her parakeet, flies from the window sill and lands on her head. She reaches up and takes the bird in her hand and kisses him on the beak. "That's my pretty bird," she says, and moves him to her shoulder. "Pretty bird! Pretty bird!" Chi-chi screeches. "Can we have some quiet please?" Grandpa yells from the living room.

I keep thinking about the student in the checkered jumper. I'm not old enough to know why girls interest me so much. I think about what the girl would look like in her underwear, and then I feel the rush of guilt and fear that I am somehow abnormal, sick in the head. I punish myself by going into Grandma's room and staring at the crucifix above her bed, the bloody Jesus suffering on the cross.

Although I don't have nails through my hands, I feel as though I'm suffering, too - caught between being a child and being grown up, not knowing how to behave. "Act your age!" grown-ups tell me. "Stop being a baby!" "You're not old enough for that!"

Grandpa Ed had trouble with his legs. It was muscular dystrophy, and it kept getting worse. The few steps up to their first floor apartment in East Haven were eventually too much for him, so my parents stepped in. They bought a small, single-level house in Ridgefield, Conn., for my grandmother and Ed, on the same street where Jane's younger daughter, Shirley, lived.

It was a difficult move for Jane, who had lived in and around New Haven for nearly 50 years. But it made sense to be living near family in their declining years. It must have been lonely for Jane, uprooted as she was from her friends in the Polish community, the Monarch Laundry and the other places she worked, and dropped down in that waspy, proper little New England town.

JANE RUDOWICZ IN BRONXVILLE, N.Y.,

IN 1959.

The family would get together at Grandma Jane's new house on holidays. By the time I was a teenager, I dreaded this. I recall Christmas there in 1963, when I was home on break from the Taft School. This was a time when Polish jokes were all the rage, and I feared I might die from humiliation and taunting if people at school were to find out that I was half Polish. And there was nothing quite so Polish as Grandma's house at Christmas.

To start with, you'd walk into the house and be assaulted with the kitchen smells of cabbage and sauerkraut; pigs-in-blankets and boiled sauerkraut and pork ribs were the traditional fare. And then there was the decor: the gaudy, over-decorated Christmas tree, the kitschy knick-knacks and porcelain statuary, the large portrait of JFK, draped in black crepe with a crucifix and a palm leaf from last Easter tucked in the edge of the frame. My cousin Paul was taking accordion lessons from Grandpa, so of course he and Grandpa have to play for us, and of course they play polkas. And then at the kitchen table Grandma and her cousin and her friends from New Haven are actually carrying on this loud conversation in Polish, as if that was necessary... I thought: My God, how do I get out of here?

Now, of course, I have an entirely different attitude about being Polish. Time and death and distance have separated me from that rich, ethnic atmosphere, and I mourn for it like lost youth.

Grandpa Ed could no longer get around without using a walker, and even then with great difficulty. He could still drive, however, once he and Grandma Jane managed to get him into the seat of his giant old Cadillac with the big fins. When they'd come to visit, Ed would stay in the car and we'd take turns going out to sit with him and to bring him a highball - whiskey and soda, no ice.

Ed had fewer pupils in Ridgefield than he'd had in New Haven, so he made up for the drop in income by repairing television sets in their home, back in the days when TVs were still worth repairing. The spare bedroom was filled with vacuum tubes, testers, solder and wire and all the tools necessary for working with electronics.

The accordion was not exactly the instrument of choice for young people in the 1970s, and the development of transistors and printed circuit boards was making television repair impractical. As the work diminished, so did Ed's health, slowly, as the 1970s gave way to the '80s.

His funeral was held in New Haven, where there were still many people who remembered "Ed Ruell and His Band." During visitations, in the parking lot behind the funeral home, my cousins and I drank beer and ate pizza out of the trunk of a car. In New Haven, it's spelled "apizza" an d pronounced "ah-BEETS." Pizza was born in New Haven in 1925, so they say. Then Aunt Shirley came out and yelled at us: "Get back in here! You're not supposed to be having a good time, this is a funeral for God's sake!"

There was a police escort to the cemetery of a dozen motorcycles and six or eight patrol cars. "My friend, the mayor, sent them," Grandma told everyone, bursting with pride. But afterward, back in Ridgefield, she had no mayor for a friend, and now no husband to help lift in and out of bed, and that house must have seemed so cold and quiet to her when all she could hear at times was the rhythm of her own breath.

I visited my grandmother in February 1986, when she was 82 years old. Since Grandpa Ed had died, she had acquired a menagerie: three

JANE RUDOWICZ, HOLDS HER FIRST
GRANDCHILD, BRODY PARKER BURROUGHS,
IN 1974.

dogs, four parakeets, two finches and a bowl of goldfish. One of the dogs, "Terry," barked a lot. Another, an ancient poodle, did nothing but follow my grandmother around. The third was a shaggy little thing, completely blind - it leaned against the walls when it walked, in search of the other two. I think the latter two were called "U" and "U2," because of Jane's scoldings: "Terry, get back in the bedroom! You, go on! And you, too!"

Looking around, I wondered if my grandmother had ever thrown anything away. The little house seemed stuffed to the rafters with all manner of junk. Tabletops supported mountains of old letters and photographs, floor space was taken up by stacks of sheet music and magazines. Cartons of slightly used wrapping paper and ribbons were crammed into closets.

In the spare bedroom where Ed had repaired television sets and radios, there were shelves with perhaps 1,000 vacuum tubes.

"Grandma, why don't you get rid of this stuff?" I asked.

"Because someday, these things will be worth something," she replied.

I argued that transistors had been invented, that this stuff was obsolete, but she just shrugged, and then I realized that the room was a shrine. Ed's picture, in a gaudy frame, rested on a table surrounded by plastic flowers and crucifixes. I should have kept my mouth shut.

Later, I offered to take her Christmas tree down. "Grandma, it's almost March," I whined.

"I'll take it down later, when someone comes to help me take it down," she said. "And if no one comes, so what? I won't have to put it up again next year."

I again offered to take it down, but she declined. "No, not yet. Maybe after Easter. I like the way it looks."

Before I left, she parted with some of her prized possessions.

"You're going to inherit them someday. You might as well take them now."

So I headed back to Pennsylvania with two Polish prayer books, a flare gun, an old electric guitar and an accordion – nothing fancy, just a plain black squeeze box that beginners would have started their lessons with.

I'd had a pleasant time those few days, visiting other relatives and sitting in Grandma Jane's kitchen, drinking coffee and pumping her for family history. But there was something disturbing happening in that house that I could not quite identify. You know that feeling, when you think you see some movement out of the corner of your eye, and when you turn quickly, there's nothing there.

But there was something there. It's just that I didn't realize what it was at the time.

On that last visit, my grandmother asked me to stay a while longer. "I can't," I said. "My wife is waiting for me at home."

She looked at me as if I'd been naughty. "You didn't tell me you got married," she said. "I didn't even know you had a girlfriend."

I was dumbstruck. "Of course I have a wife – Alice – and two kids. Grandma!

Somewhere behind those twinkling eyes, wires had crossed. I realized that she thought - at least for the moment - that she was talking to my brother, 15 years my junior.

"No, it's me, Grandma, Parker. That's my brother Phil who's still single."

Other troubling signs began to reveal themselves. The house was not just a jumble of junk. Bundles of years-old newspapers were tied with string and stacked in a low wall that snaked around the living room. In

JANE PICKASZ AT AGE 10 HOLDS A CANDLE
AND PRAYER BOOK FOR HER FIRST
COMMUNION IN 1914.

a corner behind that wall I found dried dog feces. And there were things in the refrigerator that had spoiled long ago, like the contents in a bottle of ketchup that had gone black.

I had never experienced dementia or Alzheimer's disease at the time. The old people I had known had become frail or ill and died with minds intact. This was a new experience, and one that I chose to deny, at least initially.

That following Christmas, we received a package of presents from Grandma. She had always sent odd presents - knitted objects of unknown utility, age-inappropriate clothing for the children. But these were even more puzzling. My gift was an old Hawaiian shirt that I remember Grandpa Ed wearing, and it looked as if it had not been washed.

Those were the last gifts we were to receive from her. In a card the following Christmas, she wrote that she was afraid to send gifts. And that fear she experienced at trying to recall who to send gifts to and at what stages of life those people might be in would manifest itself in yet another way.

By 1989, Grandma Jane, although physically healthy, became weaker in mind. This I heard from my cousins, who had taken over care of her from their mother, my aunt Shirley, who had moved out of the house across the street after the death of her husband, Joe.

My cousins complained that Grandma Jane had become a pack rat, hoarding all kinds of junk. They said that whenever they talked her into taking some things to the dump, she'd just fill her car with junk there and come back with twice as much. She was suspicious and resentful of my cousins, they said, for trying to steal her stuff.

I realized then that the few things she had parted with on my last visit to her had been a hugely sacrificial gesture on her part. When my 10-year-old daughter was looking for something to take to school – pictures of her ancestors – for a discussion on family heritage, we pulled the box out of the closet and looked through it. She picked up one of the prayer books, undid the clasp and leafed through the brittle yellow pages.

"What does it say? Can you read it?" she asked me.

"No, I can't even speak the words. It is our alphabet, but the letters have different sounds."

She picked up a photo of an old house and read from the back of it: "The house where we lived in Krasnik."

"Is the house still there?" she asked.

"I doubt it. There were two world wars, and millions died."

"May I take the prayer book to school?" she asked.

"Yes, but you must be very careful with it."

"Because it's old?"

"No, it's not that old," I said. "But it means so much...it's been kept..."

There was another photo in the box of Jane at age 10, in 1914, in her communion dress, holding a candle and that same prayer book. A lifetime had passed from the moment of that photo to the moment my daughter lifted the little book from the box - 75 years worth of childbirth, joy, pain and grief.

That prayer book, brought to life again, bathed once more in a little girl's breath, seemed a symbol of just how long a long life can be.

It was a typical fall morning in 1991, our sleepy and sullen children rushing through breakfast, stuffing their book bags, when the phone rang. Figuring it to be the daily call from the neighbor kid offering our son a ride, I picked up the phone and answered: "Pizza Hut."

Just silence on the other end, and then "Oh, I musta got the wrong numba..."

It wasn't the neighbor kid but I recognized the voice, that coastal Connecticut accent somewhere between New York and Boston. It was my Aunt Shirley.

"Wait, wait!" I said and apologized.

"Jeez, whatsa matter with you? It's Grandma. She died."

I found myself back at the same funeral home in New Haven, but this time there was no pizza and beer in the trunk of the car. Fewer people came this time, because Grandma Jane had outlived most of her friends. There was no police escort to the cemetery, either.

After her coffin was lowered into the pit, we stood talking quietly in small groups – my father, my cousins, a few other friends and relatives. Shirley had wandered off in the direction of her husband's grave. Joe had been a sweet, gentle man, but his death was rushed by drink.

We heard a mournful wail and our quiet conversations hung in the air.

"Oh, Joe! Why did you leave me?" Shirley cried. I watched her fall to her knees by his stone, watched her daughter Holly wrap an arm around her.

In the car going back to Ridgefield, my cousins told me Grandma stories, some of them sad tales of dementia, others funny enough to make us cramp from laughter. Like the time they showed Grandma a porno movie; I couldn't believe they would do that.

"She kept saying, 'That's too big, it can't be real, it must be fake'," my cousin Paul said.

We were still chuckling over that when we pulled into the driveway of Grandma's house, stepped around the old station wagon with flattened tires, onto the rotted deck piled high with broken lawn chairs and cracked flower pots, and into the kitchen, into which the wandering wall of newspapers and magazines had intruded.

The mess was sobering, but the shock did not hit me until I descended halfway down the darkened basement steps, reached for the string and pulled on the light.

By Thanksgiving 1991, the old station wagon had been hauled off to the junkyard and the furniture and appliances from Grandma Jane's house in Ridgefield had been donated to a local charity. I arrived that weekend with my wife and children to begin the task of cleaning the rest of the stuff out of the house. And it was a lot of stuff.

When I had descended into the basement that night of Grandma's funeral, I had no idea how far she had declined mentally in those few years. But here was evidence of an illness of astounding energy. There was no room to walk in that large basement, no room to even reach the bottom of the steps. It was everywhere four feet deep in the worthless detritus of human existence.

On that night when I first saw the basement, I noticed at least a dozen old tricycles, and 30 or 40 folding lawn chair in various states of disrepair. "She brought the tricycles and toys back from the dump," my cousin Karl explained, "so the younger brothers and sisters of Grandpa's pupils would have something to play with during the lessons. She would forget that Grandpa was dead..."

"And the lawn chairs?" I asked.

"She thought they could be repaired."

For whom? I thought.

When we waded into the cellar to begin emptying it, I found that the water pump had been leaking, and that the bottom-most layer was soaked. Mold had begun to spread over the mounds of clothing,

THIRD COUSINS IN POLAND.

SOME OF THE FRIENDS AND RELATIVES OF
MY GRANDMOTHER'S FAMILY LEFT BEHIND
IN KRASNIK, POLAND, SENT THIS PHOTO
OF THEMSELVES TO AMERICA.

lampshades, draperies and wicker baskets. She must have saved every
utility bill, every receipt she ever received, and the boxes of these had split
and spilled their contents into the gray slush. Everywhere were cardboard
boxes stuffed with used wrapping paper, ribbons and bows, damp, faded
and musty. If she had never thrown anything away in her life it would
have been bad enough, but in those last years she furiously added to her
collection with trips to the dump and to the neighbors' trash cans.

We had ordered a 30-cubic-yard Dumpster in which to dispose of
the trash. We filled it, and then we filled another. There was absolutely
nothing of value in the house. When we left early the next week, we took
only a few salvaged items: a stool, a miniature wooden wheelbarrow, a pair
of crutches and a box of old family photos and letters. Some of the photos
were of Grandma in earlier days, and in her grin and the glint of her eyes I
thought I could detect the madness that would later afflict her. I wondered
if I and my children might inherit that affliction from Grandma, too.

I lifted out some letters written in Polish, dated from the 1950s. In
one was a photo, on the back of which was written, "Third cousins." It
struck me as tragic that I probably had relatives still living in Poland,
and that only Grandma would have known who they are and where they
might be. And they would never know that she had died, or under what
circumstances, or ever know about her descendants.

It was a thought that would haunt me for years to come.

It is 1994, and I find myself in a taxi speeding on a rutted road
across the cold, gray, flat landscape of southern Poland in the dim light
of a January afternoon. I am here on other business, but I have managed
to get away from Lublin for a few hours to visit the town where my
grandmother, Jane, was born, and possibly to find those distant relatives

who share my blood.

In my hands are the letters and photos I pulled from the box amid all the junk in my grandmother's Connecticut house. We cruise the muddy streets of Krasnik and find the police station. The chief is bored on this sleepy Saturday and is delighted to have something to do, like helping me find my relations. I show him the photo of the house where she was born. He laughs.

"Let me tell you, we had this war here!" he says, and he tells me that there are no old buildings in Krasnik. I imagine the rubble of ancient homes crushed beneath tank treads.

Starobrat is the surname of my great-grandmother, and the chief knows some people by this unusual Ukrainian name. We go to their houses and talk, but it is difficult to make connections; it was so long ago.

At one house, the chief throws open the door and steps into the kitchen as if it is his own. Two old women cooking at a crude, cinder-block stove seem unsurprised. The room is overly warm and smells like my grandmother. We look through the photos and letters and come to no conclusions. The watery eyes of one of the women gaze through my eyes and into my soul. They understand why I am there; they need no detailed explanation. This is the motherland, and I am a son. Or someone's grandson.

The taxi races back toward Lublin, an in the darkness I feel nothing but disappointment at having come so close, yet learned so little. If she had only given me a name, I think. Instead, I come away with nothing.

As years passed, the connection to my Polish heritage diminished to an annual exchange of Christmas cards with Aunt Shirley. As a teenager,

"Two old women cooking at a crude, cinder-block stove... understand why I am there; they need no detailed explanation. This is the motherland, and I am a son. Or someone's grandson."

I was embarrassed by the ethnicity; as an adult, I was proud of it and regretful that my children had known none of it. But then something strange happened.

My daughter, Caitlyn, who had been living in New York for six years, moved to a new neighborhood in Brooklyn - Greenpoint. It's a neighborhood of Polish immigrants, Polish meat markets, Polish hardware stores. It's Polish you hear on the street, not English. Visiting her there was like visiting Warsaw, or the New Haven of my childhood. She loves living there. Maybe it's something in her blood.

My daughter is an adult now, although in my dreams she mostly appears as a 10-year-old – that age when she took that Polish prayer book to school. She came home recently, bringing her boyfriend, Ben, along with her.

"Do you still have that accordion from Grandma Jane's?" she asked me. Ben is a musician. He wanted to learn how to play it, she explained.

I told her that of course I still had it and went upstairs to the storage closet to look for it, thinking all the while that I really didn't want to part with this rare remembrance of my maternal line. The storage closet was crammed with boxes of who-knows-what, and the sweat beaded on my brow as, kneeling, I pulled and pushed them out of the way to reach the rear. Why had we accumulated all this stuff? I thought: Would this house be as bad as Grandma's when we died?

I emerged with the dusty black case, opened it and handed the instrument to Ben. It wheezed as he pulled the bellows, and suddenly the memories flooded my brain: Ronnie – the tall red-headed kid with the warts – taking lessons on the big blue accordion; flashes of the Lawrence Welk Show on my grandmother's TV set; Grandpa Ed and my cousin Paul entertaining family at Christmas.

"Can we take it?" my daughter asked.

I told them yes, without hesitation. The accordion was just one piece of stuff that Grandma Jane had given me, and how much did stuff really matter, anyway?

My daughter was watching Ben struggle with a melody. She smiled, and I noticed the faint blue line of a vein on her jaw, and I wondered if this scene might be a memory she would carry into her old age, every time she heard an accordion play.

Acknowledgements

Although most of the material in this book came from my own memory, research and photo collection, others deserve credit.

For "Early Bird," I relied heavily on scrapbooks and photos in the collection of the Washington County (Pa.) Historical Society, as well as "Cicero Flying Field: Origin, Operation, Obscurity and Legacy – 1891-1916," by Carroll F. Gray. And I thank Margaret Thompson for her account of her late husband's recollections of his father, and for the use of family photos.

For "Life of Enos," I am grateful for the help and information I received from the descendants of Enos Christman, particularly Florence Morrow Christman, from whose book, "One Man's Gold: The Letters and Journal of a Forty Niner," I extracted images and journal entries. The photo of the Sonora Herald office is published courtesy of the Bancroft Library, University of California.

Many of the images in "The Spirits of Lebanon" are taken from yearbooks and informational material of Darrow School, New Lebanon, N.Y. Some of the remembrances in that story and "Enter, With Torches" were shared with me by Dean Bryant Hall, who supplied the photo of his mother with the headmaster.

I am much obliged to Observer Publishing Co. for the use of its photo and newspaper archives, for employing me for so long and permitting me the time to develop and write these stories on my Web log.

And I thank all of those readers who commented on the stories and urged me to write more, particularly my wife, Alice, whose sage advice I cannot do without.